THE
IDES OF
MARCH

ASPECTS OF ANTIQUITY
Naphtali Lewis
General Editor

Greek Historical Documents:
The Fifth Century B.C., by Naphtali Lewis
The Fourth Century B.C., by John Wickersham and Gerald Verbrugghe
The Roman Principate, by Naphtali Lewis

The Golden Age of Augustus, by Meyer Reinhold
The Interpretation of Dreams and Portents, by Naphtali Lewis
Diaspora: Jews in the Greek and Roman World, by Meyer Reinhold
The Ides of March, by Naphtali Lewis

THE
IDES OF
MARCH

NAPHTALI LEWIS

Samuel Stevens & Company
Sanibel and Toronto
1985

(cataloguing in publication data)

Library of Congress Cataloging in Publication Data

Lewis, Naphtali.
    The Ides of March.

    A collection of translations of Latin texts dealing with Julius Caesar and the circumstances of his time.
    Bibliography: p.
    Includes index.
    1. Rome—History—First Triumvirate, 60–53 B.C.—Sources. 2. Rome—History—53–44 B.C.—Sources. 3. Caesar, Julius—Assassination. 4. Rome—History—Civil War, 43–31 B.C.—Sources. I. Title.
DG263.L48   1984   937'.05   84-24118
ISBN 0-89522-026-1
ISBN 0-89522-027-X (pbk.)

Samuel Stevens & Company
2840 Gulf Drive
Sanibel, Florida 33957

64 Alexandra Boulevard
Toronto, Canada M4R 1L9

U.S. Edition
ISBN 0-89522-026-1/027-X

Canadian Edition
ISBN 0-88866-626-8/627-6

Design/Maher & Murtagh

To
Lionel Casson
and
Bluma L. Trell
collegis necnon amicis

Contents

Preface

Historians of the recent past have at their disposal tons of source material: mountains of official archives, masses of private documents, complete files of newspapers and magazines — truly an *embarras de richesses* through which they must plow their way, sifting, selecting, discarding. As the distinguished biographer and critic Leon Edel remarks in a recent essay, "I do not disparage archives, I simply groan when I see one." For the historian of antiquity the situation is the exact opposite. He, or she, can consult only the works of literature, the documents [inscriptions, papyri, coins, ostraca, wooden tablets] and the monuments that have survived, mostly incomplete, the hazards of time. In this pitifully scrappy armamentarium the prober must try to track down clues like some latter-day Sherlock Holmes.

Relatively dense clusters of sources do exist for three, and only three, periods of the classical past. The first centers upon Athens from the mid-fifth to the mid-fourth century B.C. The second such cluster allows us to explore in unusual detail the age of Cicero and Caesar, the decades that witnessed the death throes of the Roman Republic. The third illuminates with equal sharpness the period immediately following, that which saw Octavian's emergence as sole ruler, his adoption of the name Augustus and his establishment of the regime he called Principate and we generally call the Roman Empire. In this volume the reader will sample the source material relating to the second of these periods, and in particular to its climactic event, the assassination of Julius Caesar.

In the Western world most people today know the Caesar story from the genius of Shakespeare, who parades before us a series of dramatic clashes of personalities. Seen in the perspective of Roman history, however, the assassination of Caesar and its sequelae were the culmination of a century of violence in Roman politics — a period that twentieth-century writers have often referred to as "The Roman Revolution." It began in 133 B.C. when a group of senators, with the pontifex maximus at their head, invaded the electoral assembly and clubbed to death Tiberius Gracchus along with 300 of his supporters. Tiberius was standing for reelection to the tribunate — an unprecedented step and therefore, in the eyes of the diehard senators, an act of revolution. Increasingly polarized thereafter, Roman society in the next generation found opposing leaders in Marius and Sulla; and in the generation after that *optimates* rallied to Cicero, Cato and, as a last resort, Pompey, while the support of the *populares* was won by the remarkable and, as events proved, unbeatable Julius Caesar. Unbeatable, but of course mortal, as the Ides of March demonstrated.

But historical perspective does not dim the drama of the Ides of March. Few events in history have exercised so firm and lasting a hold on the interest and imagination of Western civilization. Practically from the moment of its occurrence Caesar's assassination has intrigued not only historians but, even more, the public at large. Questions abound: What would have happened if Caesar had yielded to the unfavorable omens and to his wife's entreaties, and had stayed at home that day? How would the course of history have been altered if Caesar had lived and continued to rule? What if, after the assassination, Octavian had deferred to parental suasion and declined Caesar's inheritance? One noted scholar recently evoked "more nightmares still for those who have time to waste on [such] hypotheses."[1] Nevertheless the questions and speculations persist, even though (a psychologist would perhaps say, "just because") they are by their very nature unanswerable. It is as though people's minds or psyches need constant reassurance that individuals do help shape human history and are not just swept along by it.

Beyond the popular speculations lie the historical judgments. Was the assassination the elimination of a tyrant, or the murder of an enlightened and benevolent despot? The answers given to this question have varied with time and place, with the political values and loyalties of each particular writer. In 46 B.C. Cicero was more prophetic than he knew when, in appealing to Caesar for the return of Marcellus (p. 47 , below), he said, "Among generations yet unborn there will arise, as there has arisen among us, sharp disagreement. Some will surely praise your achievements to the skies, while others will perhaps discern some deficiency." By their friends and supporters, like Cicero, the conspirators were called tyrannicides and heroes. The conspirators called themselves liberators — a wishful and ironic appellation, as things turned out. Their conspiracy had an ideological target — *regnum* [monarchy]; and Caesar to them was its embodiment. But as men like Cicero and Brutus were imbued with Greek culture, "the extent to which [they] are representative of the typical Roman senator is very doubtful."[2] Not every member of the senatorial ruling class was ipso facto opposed to Caesar — far from it: many were his staunch allies, and there must surely have been, as always, a large "undistributed middle." The politics of the oligarchic republic made for some strange bedfellows, and for rapidly shifting alliances. And family ties often made stronger bonds than did vested interest or what many moderns have thought of, anachronistically, as party lines. Then, too, Roman politics had its own particular cant, its slogans and shibboleths, and these must be placed in their proper setting. For example,

"aspiration to *regnum* was an accusation too frequently repeated in the political polemics of the declining Republic to be taken at face value. It was made against Sulla and Cinna, against Catilina and Clodius. Cicero himself could not escape similar defamations. When his enemies denounced his arbitrary conduct during his consulate they spoke of his *regnum* or *tyrannis*. Thus, and only thus, ought one to interpret all the passages in Cicero's writings where Caesar, Pompey, Antony and Dolabella are characterized as tyrants."

By the same token the liberty in the name of which the conspirators rained their twenty-three dagger blows upon Caesar's body was essentially a catchword for a vague, idealized senatorial government that they apparently expected would somehow automatically come into being as soon as the tyrant had been gotten out of the way. But they had no preconcerted plan of action for attaining the desired result. When they raised aloft their bloody daggers in the senate house and proclaimed that tyranny was dead, to their amazement the other senators, instead of rallying to their cry of liberty, fled in panic, crying havoc. Losing the initiative in irresolution, the assassins were placed on the defensive as early as the day after the Ides, and less than a month later the situation at Rome had become so menacing to their personal safety that Brutus and Cassius deemed it the better part of valor to leave the city.

In modern times libertarian writers, especially in societies emerging from autocratic rule, and especially if they were philosophers rather than historians, have tended to echo Cicero's ringing rhetoric. Brutus in particular has been idealized and romanticized in one vein of modern thought as a paragon of selfless devotion to the cause of liberty, whose tragic flaw was naiveté or impracticality in the rough-and-tumble world of politics and government. But his contemporaries are likelier to have seen Brutus as an intransigent defender of class privilege, and to have remembered that in practical affairs he was not above lending money at 48% interest — four times the normal rate — to a provincial city in financial distress.

Another school of historical interpretation, proclaiming its hard-headed realism, idealizes Caesar. For over a century now this theme and its variations have held the field under the awesome aegis of Theodor Mommsen.[3] The pro-Caesarians emphasize — correctly — that the assassination was perpetrated by a motley band of envious or misguided renegades, personal enemies, and political irredentists. But when they go on to exalt Caesar as the indispensable man of the hour, and to denounce his murder as a mad act of treason, they indulge in value judgments that beg the question.

Sutor ne supra crepidem (Shoemaker, stick to your last!)[4]

is probably the wisest, certainly the safest principle to follow in wrestling with such problems of historical interpretation. Few aspects of ancient history are better documented than the pervasive moral and political corruption of the republic in its last decades: it had become, in a characterization attributed to Caesar himself, "nothing, a mere word, without substance or form." And, moral judgments aside, the fact remains that it did prove impossible for the anti-Caesarians to breathe new life into it. Such, fundamentally, were the reasons why Caesarism was not aborted by the assassination, but survived under Caesar's heir. For the great majority of Roman citizens the liberty that Brutus and Cassius prated about was a code-word for a system of government of, by and for a privileged few. It was threatened with overthrow? No amount of high-sounding talk could bring them to care. If autocracy promised them an end to the miseries of endless civil war and a share in the good life, then they were ready for autocracy. In his franker moments, those he shared with his friend Atticus, Cicero admitted as much: as the quarrel between Caesar and Pompey approached the brink of war he remarked in one of his letters [Book 7 no. 7] that neither senate, publicans, bankers nor farmers were afraid of living under a *regnum* if it meant peace. And it cannot be doubted that under the Pax Augusta that ensued, the beneficiaries of Rome's wealth and empire, while still only a small fraction of the total population, added up to a larger number of people than ever before, in a wider geographical expanse.

*

The English translations of this volume are my own. Thanks go to the following persons and institutions for supplying photographs and permission to reproduce them in the plates: for the coins, to the American Numismatic Society and curator William E. Metcalf; for the head of Pompey, to the Ny Carlsberg Glyptotek, Copenhagen, and director Flemming Johansen; and for the rest, to Fototeca Unione, Rome, and Karen Einaudi.

N.L.
Id. Mart. MDCCCCLXXXIIII.

Principal Sources

Latin Writers

GAIUS JULIUS CAESAR, 102 [or 100]-44 B.C., while making his mark principally in politics and warfare, was also the author of several works on literary as well as political and military subjects. The only works of his now extant are the *Commentaries*, i.e. accounts of *The Gallic War* and *The Civil War*, written in the third person in a style characterized by Cicero as straightforward and graceful.

MARCUS TULLIUS CICERO, 106-43 B.C., orator, politician, litterateur, has left a vivid record of the last decades of the republic, years in which he was an active supporter of Pompey in the civil war, and later of Brutus and Cassius against the partisans of the murdered Caesar. There is extant a collection of his letters, 90 addressed to him and 774 from him to various friends and acquaintances, including the leading figures of the day. For the months immediately following the Ides of March these letters provide an almost day-by-day record of his rapidly fluctuating hopes and despair. From the same period come his last great orations, the *Philippics* (the title echoing Demosthenes; fourteen are extant of an original sixteen, and two of the fourteen were not actually delivered), a barrage of savage attacks on Mark Antony from 2 September 44 to 21 April 43 B.C., which ultimately led to Cicero's proscription and death.

GAIUS SUETONIUS TRANQUILLUS, ca. A.D. 70-140, was for a time a secretary to the emperor Hadrian, which post gave him ready access to imperial archives. His *Lives of the Twelve*

Caesars [Julius to Domitian], while uncritical assemblages of fact and gossip, preserve much information of value.

VELLEIUS PATERCULUS, ca. 25 B.C.-A.D. 35, a retired army officer, wrote a *Compendium of Roman History* in two books, the second covering the period 146 B.C. - A.D. 30. For all its faults — among them, adulation of the imperial family, rhetoric, superficiality — it is our most valuable connected account in Latin of the period covered by the present volume.

Greek Writers

APPIAN, ca. A.D. 95-165, a native of Alexandria, had a career in the Roman civil service. Of his *Roman History* in twenty-four books, Books 13-17 cover a century of civil wars, 133 - 35 B.C. His work, though uncritically superficial and colored by his pro-imperial attitudes, has much information that is useful to us, especially in supplementation of other sources.

DIO CASSIUS, ca. A.D. 155-230, was born in Bithynia, the son of a Roman senator. After a public career culminating in the consulship, he retired and devoted nearly a quarter-century to composing a *History of Rome* in eighty books, from Rome's beginnings to A.D. 229. Strongly pro-imperial, uneven in quality, rhetorical in tone, peppered with personal opinions informed by no consistent historical view, the considerable surviving portions of this mammoth work are often a valuable, sometimes our only, source.

PLUTARCH, ca. A.D. 45-125, of Chaeronea in central Greece, wrote voluminously during a long life. The bulk of his enormous literary output is a collection of over sixty *Moral Essays* on a wide range of subjects. His *Parallel Lives*, a world classic, compare fifty prominent figures from Greek and Roman history, including Brutus, Caesar, Cicero, Crassus and Pompey, compared with Dion of Syracuse, Alexander the Great, Demosthenes, Nicias and Agesilaus, respectively. These are for us a prime historical source, but it must be remembered that they were not written as history but as anecdotal, hero-worshipping biography.

NICOLAUS of Damascus, born ca. 64 B.C., for a time secretary of Herod the Great (whom he accompanied to Rome), wrote a huge *Universal History*, now lost. His flattering tract on the youth of Augustus, surviving in considerable part, includes an account of the conspiracy against and assassination of Julius Caesar.

Who Was Who

AHENOBARBUS ["Red-beard"]
Lucius Domitius Ahenobarbus, -48 B.C. Scion of an old, wealthy and powerful aristocratic family, he was notable for his arrogance and vice in a dissolute age. He married Cato's sister. Spared by Caesar early in the civil war, he rejoined Pompey and fell at Pharsalus. The emperor Nero was his great-great-grandson.

ANTONY
Marcus Antonius, 83-30 B.C. His career as a Caesarian began in 54 B.C., when he became one of Caesar's lieutenants in the Gallic war. As tribune of the people in January of 49 B.C. he vetoed the motion that would have recalled Caesar, stripping him of his command. He fought at Pharsalus, and the following year Caesar, when named dictator, appointed Antony his "master of horse." In 44 B.C. he was Caesar's colleague in the consulship. After Philippi there ensued between him and Octavian a twelve-year rivalry and struggle for sole control, which ended in Octavian's victory at Actium and Antony's subsequent suicide in Alexandria.

ATTICUS ["the Athenian"]
Titus Pomponius Atticus, 109-32 B.C. A wealthy eques who stayed out of politics, he was able to associate with most of the prominent men of his day. We know him principally as the close friend and financial adviser of Cicero, whose extant letters to him number some 400 (nearly half the total of Cicero's extant correspondence) ranging from 68 to late in 44 B.C.

BALBUS

Lucius Cornelius Balbus. A native of Cadiz, he served in Spain under Pompey, who granted him Roman citizenship and brought him to Rome. There he joined Caesar's staff, and soon became a key aide. He was Caesar's go-between in arranging the "First Triumvirate," and his principal agent at Rome when Caesar was away during the civil war. When [in 56 B.C.] political enemies challenged in court the validity of his Roman citizenship, he was defended by Cicero (the speech is extant) and acquitted. Octavian ultimately rewarded his long years of loyal service with a consulship in 40 B.C.

BRUTUS, D.

Decimus Junius Brutus Albinus, ca. 80-43 B.C. Entrusted by Caesar with important commands in the Gallic and civil wars, he held the governorship of Transalpine Gaul for three years, returning to Rome in 45 B.C. Caesar then designated him to be governor of Cisalpine Gaul in 44-43, and consul with Plancus in 42. The reason why such a favorite of Caesar — even named secondary heir in Caesar's will — joined the conspiracy remains unclear.

BRUTUS, M.

Marcus Junius Brutus, 83-42 B.C. The son of Servilia, who had been one of Caesar's mistresses, he was pardoned by Caesar after Pharsalus. The fact that Cato the Younger was both his uncle and his wife's father may have provided a personal motive for his participation in the conspiracy against Caesar.

CASSIUS

Gaius Cassius Longinus, 83-42 B.C. As quaestor in Crassus' disastrous expedition against Parthia, he distinguished himself by successfully leading the surviving remnant of the Roman army back to Antioch. In command of a fleet off Sicily, he surrendered to Caesar soon after the battle of Pharsalus. Caesar named him and Marcus Brutus to be praetors in 44 B.C. and consuls in 41.

CATO "UTICENSIS"

Marcus Porcius Cato, 95-46 B.C. Great-grandson of Cato the Censor (and hence sometimes referred to as "the

Younger"), he was celebrated as a paragon of moral virtue. The leading spirit of the most intransigent optimates, he sided with Pompey against Caesar. After Pharsalus he fled to the Pompeian remnant in North Africa. There, at Utica, when surrender to Caesar was imminent, he spent the night reading Plato's *Phaedo* on the immortality of the soul, then took his own life. The epithet Uticensis celebrated the fame he thereby gained as the ancient exponent of "Give me liberty or give me death." Porcia [or Portia], Marcus Brutus' wife, was his sister.

CICERO

Marcus Tullius Cicero, 106-43 B.C. He first gained prominence in 70 B.C., when he successfully prosecuted Gaius Verres for high crimes committed during his governorship of Sicily. Cicero attained the consulship in 63 B.C. In doing so he was what the Romans called a "new man" in high political office — i.e. one not born into one of the families of the oligarchic nobility — but, like many a parvenu since, he became a most vociferous defender of the privileges of the class into which he had made his way. His voluminous writings — letters, orations, essays on philosophical and rhetorical subjects — survive in good part and are our principal source for the period of history covered by this volume. See further under Principal Sources.

CLODIUS

Publius Clodius Pulcher, -52 B.C. Born into the patrician family of the Claudii, he adopted the Clodius spelling of the plebeian branch to dramatize his espousal of populist politics. How many of the stories about him as a raffish cut-up are true and how many fabricated for political propaganda purposes, we shall never know. As tribune in 58 B.C. he instigated the banishment of Cicero. He led a gang in the street riots of the following years, and was finally done to death by Milo's pro-senatorial gang.

DOLABELLA

Publius Cornelius Dolabella, ca. 70-43 B.C. Though married in 50 B.C. to Cicero's daughter — he was her third husband, she was his second wife, and she divorced him after two or three years because he continued in his profligate ways — he promptly joined Caesar's side at the outbreak of the civil war. He was rewarded with a tribuneship in 47 B.C., and was designated to succeed to the consulship when Caesar should leave for the Parthian war in 44 B.C. He assumed the office after Caesar's assassination, then obtained Syria as his province for the following year and hastened there to forestall Cassius. He was defeated by Cassius, however, and knowing he could expect no mercy he committed suicide.

LEPIDUS

Marcus Aemilius Lepidus, ca. 85-13 B.C. He was praetor in 49 B.C., governor of Hither Spain in 48-47, and Caesar's colleague in the consulship of 46. Also in that year Caesar, when named dictator, appointed him his "master of horse." Soon after the assassination Lepidus secured his election as pontifex maximus in succession to Caesar, then returned to his provinces of Gaul and Spain, whence he emerged to join Antony and Octavian in the Second Triumvirate. After Philippi he remained in his province of Africa till 36 B.C., when he tried to wrest Sicily from Octavian. The latter defeated him, stripped him of all his powers, but let him live out his natural life as pontifex maximus.

MARK ANTONY: see ANTONY

MILO

Titus Annius Milo Papinianus, -48 B.C. He was the optimates' counterpart to Clodius. As tribune in 57 B.C. he was active in bringing about Cicero's recall from exile. After his gang killed Clodius he was tried and, facing conviction in spite of a casuistical but futile defense by Cicero, he went into exile at Marseilles, even then famed for its culinary delights. He was killed on returning to Italy during the civil war.

OPPIUS

Gaius Oppius, ca. 100- ca. 30 B.C. Born into an equestrian family of Roman bankers, he became with Balbus the leading manager of Caesar's affairs from 54 B.C. on. After the assassination he continued to be active in support of Octavian. His writings — biographies, probably including one of Caesar — have not survived. An ancient tradition crediting him with the authorship of "Caesar's" commentaries on the Alexandrian, African and Spanish wars is today generally regarded as being groundless: see also Principal Sources, under Caesar.

PLANCUS

Lucius Munatius Plancus was in the Gallic and civil wars a loyal lieutenant of Caesar, who rewarded him with nomination to a governorship in 44-43 B.C. and a consulship, as colleague of Decimus Brutus, in 42. Unlike the latter, he survived, by shifting with the political winds, to hold that office.

Chronology of Significant Events

B.C.

60   The "First Triumvirate," consisting of Caesar, Crassus and Pompey, is formed [*July-August*]. Caesar is elected consul for 59.

59   Caesar's agrarian law provides land for Pompey's veterans and the poor. Caesar marries Calpurnia (his fourth wife), Pompey marries Julia, Caesar's daughter [*ca. April*], and Caesar draws a new will naming Pompey his heir. Bypassing the senate Caesar has a law passed in the assembly giving him a five-year command as governor of Cisalpine Gaul and Illyricum with an army of three legions; the overawed senate adds Transalpine Gaul with the legion stationed there.

58   Caesar begins the conquest of the Gallic tribes beyond the Roman province. Cicero is driven into exile in a political reprisal by the Caesarians led by the tribune Clodius [*March*]. Clodius overreaches himself vis-à-vis Pompey, who begins [*May*] to work for Cicero's recall.

57   Bloody political street-fighting in Rome. A bill is finally passed [*4 August*] for the recall of Cicero, who returns in triumph [*4 September*]. Pompey is given empire-wide control of Rome's grain supply for five years.

56   Political violence and maneuvering continue, increasing strains in the Triumvirate. The three meet at Luca [*April*] and paper over the cracks in their disintegrating alliance. The new agreement calls for Crassus and

Pompey to be consuls in 55, followed by five-year commands in Syria and Spain respectively, and for Caesar's command, with the army that he had increased in the Gallic campaigns to eight legions, to be extended for another five years, after which he is to pass directly from his province to a second consulship. Under these terms the position of Caesar is clearly the strongest.

55 Crassus and Pompey are consuls. With Gaul pacified Caesar invades Germany and Britain. He also begins to publish his account of the Gallic war, and writes a treatise on style which he dedicates to Cicero. Crassus prepares to go to his province and wage war on Parthia.

54 Julia dies in childbirth [*September*], breaking the last bond between Pompey and Caesar. Political corruption reaches new heights, as intrigue and violence continue. Pompey, remaining at Rome, is widely thought to be striving for appointment as dictator.

53 Crassus invades Parthia and is defeated and killed at Carrhae [*June*]. Pompey, rejecting Caesar's offer of a new matrimonial alliance, marries Crassus' widow. Consular elections are postponed because of bloody clashes and riots, climaxed

52 by the murder of Clodius by Milo and his gang [*12 January*]. Gaul erupts in a general revolt against Caesar and Roman rule [*23 January*]. With Rome in the grip of anarchy, martial law is declared and Pompey is appointed sole consul, and his command in Spain, with its powerful Roman army, is extended for five years. Milo is tried for murder and exiled, despite Cicero's speech in his defense [*7 April*]. Vercingetorix is besieged by Caesar in Alesia and starved into surrender [*August-September*]; the senate votes twenty days of thanksgiving for Caesar's victory.

51 Cicero, named governor of Cilicia, reluctantly leaves Rome [*June*]. Anti-Caesarian maneuvers increase in the senate, culminating [*29 September*] in a decree that the question of appointing a successor to Caesar be definitely settled the following March 1st. Caesar snuffs

out Gallic resistance and proclaims the annexation of all Gaul to the Roman province [*December*].

50 At Rome political thrusts and counterthrusts continue between the senate and the supporters of Caesar. Decrees that Caesar give up his command the following year are vetoed one after another till a compromise is passed [by 370 to 22; *1 December*] requiring Pompey as well as Caesar to resign his command. The consul Marcellus, unilaterally exceeding his constitutional authority, authorizes Pompey to raise troops against Caesar [*3 December*], who reacts by assembling some of his troops at Ravenna and summoning two legions from Transalpine Gaul. Cicero, returning from Cilicia, repeatedly urges compromise with Caesar as infinitely preferable to civil war [*15-25 December*]. From Ravenna Caesar sends [*27 December*] a final proposal for compromise, which reaches Rome in time for

49 the senate meeting of January 1st. Rejecting compromise the senate votes [*2 January*] to declare Caesar a public enemy if he does not give up his command on or before March 1st. The tribunes Mark Antony and Quintus Cassius veto the bill. After the consuls threaten them with violence they flee from Rome to Caesar, as the senate decrees martial law [*7 January*]. Caesar responds by crossing the Rubicon: "The die is cast" [*12 January*]. Caesar sweeps down the east coast of Italy, forcing Pompey and his active supporters to abandon Rome [*17 January*], then Italy [*17 March*]. Cicero leaves to join him [*7 June*]. In a campaign of forty days Caesar crushes the Pompeian forces in Spain [*2 August*], then goes on to conquer Farther Spain and break the resistance of Marseilles [*late October*], where word reaches him from Rome that he has been named dictator. He returns to Rome, is elected consul for 48 and resigns the dictatorship [*December*].

48 Caesar's second consulship. He crosses the Adriatic [*4 January*], is joined by Antony with reinforcements [*early April*]. After Pompey wins several indecisive victories and rejects several peace offers from Caesar

[*January-July*], he is crushed in the decisive battle fought at Pharsalus in Thessaly [*9 August*]. Pompey flees to Egypt, where he is murdered [*September*]. Stopping en route to visit Troy, Ephesus and Rhodes, Caesar arrives at Alexandria [*2 October*], where he learns of Pompey's death, secures Cleopatra upon the Egyptian throne, and is attacked by the local army [*late October*]. Caesar enters his second dictatorship [*dictator II*], which lasts until April of 46 B.C.

47 The Alexandrian forces submit to Caesar [*27 March*], who takes a two-month cruise on the Nile with Cleopatra then leaves [*late June*] to settle affairs in Judaea and Syria (where he pardons Brutus and Cassius), and punish King Pharnaces of Pontus [*"Veni, vidi, vici," 2 August*]. He returns to Rome [*early October*], attends to urgent matters, then leaves with six legions to fight the Pompeian army of fourteen legions assembled in Africa [*arrival there late December*].

46 Caesar's third consulship. He defeats the Pompeians decisively at Thapsus, and Cato the Younger commits suicide [*6, 12 April*]. On receiving the news of his victory the senate proclaims [*late April*] a thanksgiving of forty days and extends his dictatorship for ten years [*dictator III*]. Caesar returns to Rome [*25 July*] and celebrates [*late August-late September*] a quadruple triumph for his victories in Gaul, Egypt, Pontus and Africa (no mention of Pharsalus, a victory over a Roman citizen). He enacts various laws, including the reform of the calendar, dedicates new public buildings, and pardons many of Pompey's supporters. Cleopatra arrives in Rome with their infant son, Caesarion. As word comes from Spain that Pompey's sons, Gnaeus and Sextus, are preparing to renew the war, Caesar speeds there on horseback in twenty-six days [*December*].

45 Caesar's fourth consulship and last military campaign. The Pompeian forces in Spain are decisively defeated at Munda [*17 March*]; Gnaeus Pompey is killed in the aftermath but Sextus escapes to conduct a guerrilla

war. Caesar completes his account of *The Civil War*. On receiving the news of Munda the senate votes a thanksgiving of fifty days, renews Caesar's dictatorship [*dictator IIII*], and gives him the permanent and hereditary title of Imperator [*late April*]. He returns to Rome, where he draws a new will making Octavius his heir [*13 September*], and celebrates a triumph [his fifth] for the victory in Spain [*October*], proclaims a general amnesty, pursues his legislative program and plans military campaigns to strengthen the eastern frontiers of the empire.

44 Caesar's fifth consulship. The senate bestows additional honors and names him *dictator perpetuus*, "dictator for life" [*February*]. He is assassinated by conspirators on March 15th, the Ides of March. The senate [*17 March*] decrees amnesty for the assassins but ratifies Caesar's acts and grants a public funeral, at which [*20 March*] the consul Antony so inflames the populace against the self-styled "liberators" that Brutus and Cassius have to run for their lives [*early April*]. Cleopatra also leaves Rome, to return to Egypt. Antony dominates the scene in and about Rome until Octavius, acclaimed all along his route from Brundisium to Rome, arrives and formally accepts his adoption as Caesar's son and heir [*early May*]. After initial hostility Antony and Octavian appear to be reconciled [*early August*], but are soon again at odds and go about collecting separate armies [*October*]. Cicero, meanwhile, has begun [*2 September*] the famous series of *Philippic* orations against Antony, whose next move is to march his legions to Cisalpine Gaul and besiege Decimus Brutus in Mutina [*December*].

43 Consuls: Aulus Hirtius and Gaius Vibius Pansa. The senate adopts [*early January*] the strategy, urged by Cicero, of supporting Octavian as a means of destroying Antony. Octavian and the consuls march against Antony, who is driven from Mutina in two battles [*14, 21 April*] which cost both consuls their lives. Antony goes to Transalpine Gaul, where he joins Lepidus [*late May*]. Octavian demands to be named consul [*early*

July], and when the senate refuses he marches on Rome and has himself and his cousin Quintus Pedius elected [*19 August*]. Cicero, disillusioned of his dream of using and then discarding Octavian, leaves Rome, never to return. Recognizing that cooperation would now be mutually advantageous, Octavian, Antony and Lepidus meet near Bononia in Cisalpine Gaul [*November*], and agree to form the "Second" Triumvirate, to proscribe their principal political and personal enemies, and to divide the rule of the empire among themselves. The three return to Rome, enter the city with armed forces, and a law is passed [*27 November*] naming them "triumvirs for restoring the republic" with proconsular power for five years. Cicero is among the first to be killed in the proscription [*7 December*].

42   Consuls: Marcus Aemilius Lepidus and Lucius Munatius Plancus. Caesar is officially declared by the senate and people to be a god [*early January*]. Antony and Octavian prepare to pursue and punish Brutus and Cassius while Lepidus stays behind to guard the home front. They cross the Adriatic with twenty-eight legions and move east, while Brutus and Cassius, with nineteen legions plus 13,000 allied cavalry and 4,000 mounted archers, move westward from the Hellespont. The armies meet at Philippi in Macedonia. Cassius commits suicide after the first battle [*23 October*], even though it is indecisive, Brutus after the second [*mid-November*], which is decisive.

I

THE VICTOR

From the First Triumvirate to Pharsalus [60-48 BC]

Pompey wanted no one to be his equal in authority.
— Caesar, *The Civil War* i.4

The leaders' distinction was about equal
. . . and the issue hard to judge because there was
something to favor on either side.
— Cicero, *The Speech for Ligarius* vi.19

Caesar could now brook no superior, Pompey no equal.
— Lucan, *Pharsalia* i.125-6

1

The First Triumvirate

In the middle of the year 60 B.C. three important figures in Roman politics found their several ambitions frustrated by the Senate's successful manipulation of the governmental machinery. Pompey the Great [Gnaeus Pompeius Magnus], recently returned from a series of spectacular military successes in the eastern Mediterranean, sought for his veterans the by now traditional land allotments that they expected; but the Senate, unwilling to see Pompey's prestige and political power further enhanced, prevented the passage of the land bill. Marcus Licinius Crassus, extraordinarily rich and politically restive, had saved Rome from the revolt of the Spartacus-led gladiators in 71 B.C., had been elected with Pompey to the consulship of the following year, and had been wallowing politically ever since. Younger than these two, Gaius Julius Caesar, having financed his budding political career with extensive loans advanced by Crassus, had just returned from a praetorship in Spain to find the Senate obstructing his bid for the consulate, the next step up the political ladder.

Under these conditions Caesar, who appears to have taken the initiative, had little difficulty in persuading Pompey and Crassus of the mutual benefits derivable for their supporters and for their own careers from a pooling of their influence and resources: Pompey contributed the backing of his citizen soldiery, Crassus his wealth, Caesar his popularity with the plebs as well as important family ties with members of the senatorial nobility. Thus was formed what we, in modern times, call the First Triumvirate. It should be noted, however, that — unlike the later Second Triumvirate (p. 136), which had itself openly proclaimed and legally constituted (by, it is true, a cowed and complaisant Senate) — the coalition of Pompey, Crassus and Caesar was a "shadow cabinet" operating behind the scenes. Though unavowed, its existence was manifest from its acts, and its extralegal status was no impediment to the control of the Roman government exercised for the next half-dozen years by this "three-headed creature," as the contemporary writer Varro dubbed it.

Cicero, *Letters to Atticus*, Book 2, no. 3

[Somewhere in the country, December 60 B.C.]

. . . Now as to January and my *attitude politique* . . . .[5] It is certainly something to be pondered. Either I strenuously oppose the agrarian law, which means something of a fight, but a most laudatory one; or I do nothing, which is no different from going off to Solonium or Antium; or I support it, as they say Caesar confidently expects me to. Cornelius was here — I mean Balbus, Caesar's henchman. He assured me that Caesar will follow my advice and Pompey's in everything, and will make an effort to bring Pompey and Crassus together again. The considerations on this side are my intimate connection with Pompey and, if I want it, with Caesar as well, reconciliation with my political opponents, peace with the populace, and quiet in my old age. But I still feel strongly, as I wrote in that *envoi* of Book Three,[6]

> Meanwhile the goals which from the start of youth
> As consul too you sought with heart and soul,
> Hold fast, while good men praise and raise your fame.

As Calliope herself inspired these verses in a book full of *sentiments nobles*, I don't think I should waver in believing that "the one best omen is to fight for one's fatherland."[7]

Dio Cassius, *Roman History*, Book 37, chapters 50-57

Stymied by [the consul] Metellus and the others [i.e. senators], Pompey . . . realized that he had no real power: he had only the name and the envy generated by his former power, but derived no benefit therefrom. He regretted that he had discharged his legions prematurely, thus delivering himself into his enemies' hands. . . .

During these events in the city Caesar had been governor of Lusitania, where he could with little difficulty have suppressed the brigandage (which was practically chronic there) and then rested on his laurels, but that was not his way.

3

Eager for glory, emulating Pompey and the others before him who had once wielded great power, he entertained no small purposes but hoped that, if he accomplished something big, he would be elected consul at once and would go on to extraordinary achievements. His hope was encouraged in particular by the fact that at Cadiz, when quaestor, he had dreamt that he was enjoying intercourse with his mother, which, he learned from the seers, meant that he would wield great power. . . .[8]

Caesar subjugated the Lusitanians of the Herminian mountains.[9] Thinking this accomplishment had provided him with a sufficient stepping-stone to the consulship, without waiting for his successor to arrive he set out in haste for the elections, determined to seek the office before celebrating his triumph. . . . He entered the city and announced his candidacy. While he canvassed others he paid court especially to Pompey and Crassus, and although there was still mutual hostility between them and each had his own political following (so that each opposed what he saw the other wanted), Caesar won them over and was elected by all of them with one accord. This indeed is evidence of his exceptional political skill, that he appreciated the opportunity and so managed the measure of his attendance upon them as to attach them both to himself even though they were working against each other.

Not content with this, he actually reconciled the men themselves, not because he wanted them to be of one mind but because he saw that they were very powerful and he realized that without the support of one or both he would never wield great power. On the other hand, if he associated himself with either one of them alone he would thereby make the other his opponent, who would then be the source of griefs far outweighing the successes gained with the other's support. It seemed to him that men are always readier to do in their enemies than to work with their friends. . . .

With this in mind Caesar began to court them and eventually reconciled them with each other. He reckoned that without them he could never attain real power and would surely at some time offend one or the other of them; and he had no fear that they would combine to become stronger than himself. He fully intended first to master others with the aid of their friendship, and a little later to master each of them with the assistance of the other. And that is how it came to pass. Once they set out to do it, Pompey and Crassus quickly made peace, each for his own private reasons, and they took Caesar into their political partnership. Pompey, wielding less power than he had expected, and seeing Crassus' influence extensive and Caesar's rising, was afraid he might be altogether sidetracked by them; but he also hoped that in partnership with them he would, through them, regain his pristine authority. Crassus counted on surpassing all by virtue of his family and fortune, and as he was far inferior to Pompey and thought Caesar would rise to great power, he wanted to set them against each other, so that neither of them would come out on top. He figured that they would be evenly matched adversaries, and that in that situation he would profit from the friendship of both and would be honored above either. Thus, he avoided aligning himself completely with the populace or with the senate, but did everything with an eye to increasing his own influence. That is why he sided with Pompey and Caesar alike, and avoided friction with either, supporting the legislative programs of both to the point where he would receive credit for whatever went according to the wishes of the one or the other, but would not be blamed for the failures.

For these reasons, then, the three formed their alliance, ratifying it with oaths. Together they controlled the public business, granting to themselves or obtaining from one another what they desired or were impelled to by circumstances.

Plutarch, *Life of Crassus*, chapters 1-7

Marcus Crassus was the son of a man who had been censor and had celebrated a triumph, but he was brought up with his two brothers in a simple abode. His brothers took wives while their parents were still alive and all trooped to the same table — which explains in good part why he was always temperate and moderate in his manner of life. When one of his brothers died he married the widow and had his children by her, and in these relations too his life was

5

no less orderly than that of any Roman. Even so, when on in years he was accused of consorting with Licinia, one of the Vestal Virgins, and she was even prosecuted by one Plotius. Now, Licinia owned a fine suburban property that Crassus wanted to acquire at a low price, and that was the reason he was always hanging around and cultivating the woman and ended up under the suspicion mentioned. . . .

It was said among the Romans that Crassus' many virtues were overshadowed by a single vice, his avarice; and that one vice, it appears, grew ever stronger in him, obscuring his other vices. The clearest proofs of his avarice are found in the size of his estate and the way he acquired it. At the start he was worth no more than three hundred talents. Then, during his consulship he sacrificed a tenth of his worth to Hercules, feasted the populace, provided each Roman citizen with a three months' supply of food, and even so, when inventorying his estate in preparation for his Parthian expedition [fifteen years later], found that he still had a worth of 7,100 talents.[10]

The greatest part, to tell the slanderous truth, was amassed from fires and wars: public calamities provided his greatest revenues. When Sulla captured the city and kept selling off the properties of the men he had killed, Crassus . . . never shrank from buying and acquiring these spoils of war, as he regarded and called them. In addition, observing that the weight and crowding together of buildings made fires and collapses everyday disasters at Rome, he kept buying slaves trained as architects and builders. Then, when he had more than five hundred of these, he would buy up houses on fire and those adjoining, which their owners in fear and uncertainty would let go at low prices. As a result, a major part of Rome became his property. Yet, though he owned so many artisans he built himself nothing but his private house. . . .

He owned numerous silver mines and very valuable lands, together with the manpower to work them, but one might reckon all this as nothing compared with the value of the many slaves he possessed of various skills — readers, secretaries, silversmiths, stewards, table-servants. He attended to their training in person, supervising and teaching them, for he believed a master's principal concern was to care for his slaves as living implements of household economy. . . .[11]

Crassus was hospitable to strangers, his house open to all. He would lend money to his friends without interest but, as he would relentlessly demand repayment by the borrower when the time had expired, his bounty became more invidious than high interest. At his banquets the company consisted mostly of plebeians and common people, and the inexpensive table afforded an unadorned good cheer that was more pleasurable than a lavish spread.

In cultural matters he devoted himself principally to practical rhetoric. He became outstanding among Rome's foremost speakers, surpassing by assiduous practice those with the best natural gifts. According to common report there was no case so small or disdained that he came to it unprepared, and in fact quite often when Pompey or Caesar or Cicero shied away he performed the pleadings. Thus he gained greater popularity, with a reputation for care and help. He was popular also for his friendly and unaffected handshakes and greetings, for he never met any Roman, however, obscure and lowly, without returning his greeting and calling him by name. He is said also to have been very learned in history, and attracted to Aristotelian philosophy. . . .

Crassus showed himself an eager supporter of Sulla in his campaigns. And from those exploits, they say, came the first beginnings of his conflict and rivalry with Pompey for fame. Pompey was younger than he, and was the son of a father held in contempt at Rome and hated with the utmost hate by the citizens. But in the events of that time Pompey shone forth and loomed so great that Sulla would stand up at his approach, uncover his head, and address him as *imperator* — honors he very seldom accorded to older men and his own equals.

All this inflamed and stung Crassus, though he was not unreasonably held in lower esteem: he lacked experience and his feats were robbed of their influence by his fatal innate vices, avarice and niggardliness. For example, it seems that, after taking Tuder, a town in Umbria, he appropriated most of the spoils, and he was denounced to Sulla for it. But in the battle for Rome, the biggest and last

7

of all, while Sulla was worsted, his units pushed back and crushed, Crassus on the right wing was victorious and pursued the enemy till nightfall, then sent a dispatch to Sulla in which he requested food for his soldiers' dinner at the same time that he told of his success. But in the ensuing proscriptions and confiscations he lost his reputation again by buying important properties at trifling prices and also asking Sulla for free grants of property. He is even said to have proscribed a man in Bruttium without Sulla's order, purely for his own profit; and as a result Sulla despised him and never again entrusted him with any public business.

Crassus' cleverness at working on people — all kinds of people — with flattery was unparalleled, but in return he was himself an easy prey to flattery from all. Another idiosyncracy reported is that this man of unequaled avarice hated and reviled his likes.

It galled him that Pompey was so successful in his campaigns, that he celebrated a triumph even before becoming a senator, and that he was publicly proclaimed Magnus, that is "Great." Once even, when someone said, "Here comes Pompey the Great," he laughed and asked, "How big?" Despairing of equaling Pompey militarily he immersed himself in politics, where, by helping people with legal services and loans, and helping candidates in canvassing and rallying supporters, he acquired influence and reputation rivaling those that Pompey derived from his many great campaigns. There was this peculiar twist in the situation: Pompey's fame and power in the city were greater when he was away on his campaigns, but when present he was often inferior to Crassus. For Pompey, majestic in his manner of living, shunned the masses, avoided the forum, helped but few who asked his help (and then grudgingly), reserving the peak of his influence for his own interests; whereas Crassus was ever ready to be of service, never aloof, always accessible, always in the midst of things. Thus his universal assistance overcame Pompey's hauteur. But in dignity of person, persuasiveness of speech and attractiveness of appearance they were equally advantaged.

Still, this rivalry never carried Crassus away to the point

of enmity or malice. He was indeed vexed that Pompey and Caesar were esteemed above him, yet his ambition was never tainted by malevolence or malignancy. . . . When Caesar was leaving for Spain as praetor and his creditors descended upon him and seized his equipage because he could not pay them, Crassus did not look the other way but obtained his release by going surety for 830 talents.

Now Rome was divided among three forces, Pompey's, Crassus' and Caesar's. . . . The sober, conservative sort in the city favored Pompey, the volatile and easily swayed trooped behind Caesar's hopes, and Crassus held the middle ground, capitalizing on both sides by constantly changing policy. He was neither a firm friend nor an implacable enemy, but readily abandoned both favor and anger to expediency. As a result he often appeared within a short time now as supporter and now as opponent of the same men and the same measures. His influence rested on favors and fear, but mostly on fear.

Cicero, *Letters to Atticus*, Book 2, no. 21
[Rome, summer 59 B.C.]
What's the use of mincing words about the political situation? The republic is finished, completely. The situation is worse than when you left to the extent that then it seemed that the state bore the weight of an absolutism of a kind that the populace enjoyed and, while irksome to sober citizens, was not pernicious; but now suddenly it is so universally detested[12] that I shudder to think how it may strike out. We have already experienced the wrath and arrogance of those [triumvirs]. In their anger at Cato they have ruined everything. But in the past they seemed to be using such slow poisons that it looked as if we would be able to die without pain. Now, however, I am afraid they have been riled by the hisses of the crowd,[13] the outspoken opinions of respectable citizens, and the grumbling of Italy. . . . If only people could have waited for the storm [i.e. the triumvirate] to pass. But although they sighed in private for a time, they presently began to groan aloud, and most recently they have all begun to speak up and shout. And so our illustrious friend [Pompey], not used to unpopularity, always accustomed to praise, abounding

in glory, is now marred in his public image, broken in spirit, and doesn't know which way to turn. He sees that to continue [his alliance with Caesar] is dangerous, to withdraw from it a sign of shilly-shally. He has turned the sober citizenry against him, and has not won over the rabble. . . .

2

Cicero's Exile and Recall

Cicero's opposition to agrarian legislation was cleverly silenced by the tribune Clodius, Caesar's man, who introduced a bill exiling anyone who put a Roman citizen to death without trial. Though couched in general terms (bills of attainder having been forbidden ever since The Twelve Tables), the law was obviously aimed at Cicero for his actions against the Catilinarian conspirators in his consulship [63 B.C.]. In May of 58 B.C. Cicero left Italy and retired first to Thessalonica and then to Dyrrhacium, just across the Adriatic, in case he obtained his hoped-for return. The political situation in Rome was so fluid that after eleven months Pompey, who had done nothing to prevent Cicero's exile, backed a bill for his recall in an effort to combat Caesar's rapidly growing influence.

Cicero, *Letters to Atticus,* Book 4, no. 1
This letter was obviously written by Cicero shortly after his return from exile.

[Rome, September 57 B.C.]
. . . It was you who were most bitter at my being exiled, and who devoted the most energy, zeal, perseverance and effort to bringing about my return. . . . The one thing wanting to complete my happiness is the sight of you, or rather your embrace. . . .

When I reached Rome the steps of the temples were filled from top to bottom with the populace, who expressed their congratulations with thunderous applause. A like crowd and like applause accompanied me right up to the Capitol, and in the forum and on the Capitol itself the crowd was prodigious.

The next day, September 5th, in the senate house I gave

thanks to the senate. On that day and the next the price of grain was at an all-time high and crowds ran first to the theater and then to the senate house, shouting, at Clodius' instigation, that the shortage of grain was my fault. On the same days the senate met on the subject, and optimates as well as populace called for Pompey to be given charge of the grain supply. As he himself was eager for the appointment and the people asked for me specifically to propose it, I did so, defining it in precise terms. . . . A decree was then passed, as proposed by me, to discuss with Pompey his taking the matter in hand, and to pass a law on the subject. . . . The next day the consuls introduced a law giving Pompey complete charge of the grain supply in the whole [Roman] world for five years. . . .

Cicero, *Letters to Atticus*, Book 4, no. 3

[Rome, 23 November 57 B.C.]

I am sure you want to know what's going on here. . . .

On the 11th as I was going down the Sacred Way, Clodius and a gang of his followed me. Shouts, stones, clubs, swords, all without warning. I stepped aside into Tettius Damio's vestibule, and the men with me easily kept his ruffians out. . . .

On the 12th he tried to set fire to Milo's house, the one on the Cermalus. Around 11 o'clock, in broad daylight, using Publius Sulla's house as his headquarters for the attack, he brought up his men, some with shields and drawn swords, others with firebrands. Then a gallant band led by Quintus Flaccus sallied forth from Milo's compound and killed the most notorious of Clodius' whole gang. He wanted to get Clodius too, but he hid inside Sulla's house. . . .

On the 19th Milo came into the Campus Martius before midnight with a large band. Clodius, although he had picked gangs of runaway slaves, did not dare go there. Milo stayed there till noon,[14] to people's great delight and his very great glory. . . .

It is now three in the morning on the 23rd as I write this. Milo has again taken possession of the Campus. . . . Clodius' side complain that I am the brains behind it all, not realizing how great are that heroic man's own courage and intelligence. His bravery is marvelous. I skip over some of his inspired new moves, but here is the gist of it. I don't think the elections will be held, and I expect that Clodius will be indicted by Milo — unless he is killed first, for if he encounters him in a riot Milo will kill him with his own hands. He won't hesitate to do it, in fact he says so openly. . . .

3

The Triumvirate Falls Apart
[56-50 B.C.]

**Dio Cassius, *Roman History*, Book 39,
chapters 25-27**

Pompey attempted to persuade the consuls not to read out
Caesar's letters right away but to conceal [the news of his
victories in Gaul] as long as possible, till the glory of his
deeds spread by itself. He also urged them to send someone to succeed Caesar in his command even before the
proper time. He was consumed by such enormous envy
that he disparaged and tried to undo everything that
Caesar had gained with his assistance. It galled him that
Caesar was so highly praised as to overshadow his own
exploits, and he blamed the populace because they slighted
him and had ears for no one but Caesar. It riled him especially to see that they remembered a man's previous
accomplishments only so long as nothing new supervened;
that they, bored with the usual, delighting in the novel,
were easily carried away by every new achievement, even
if a lesser one than the preceding; that they were impelled
by envy to cast down everything once esteemed, and by
hopes to join in exalting a rising star. Nettled by all this
and unable to have his way with the consuls, he saw Caesar
outstripping their alliance, and he could not take that lightly.
He realized that the two things that destroyed friendships
were fear and envy, and that these fail to arise when —
and only when — glory and power are equal. As long as
men have equal shares of these their friendship is firm,
but when one is raised up any higher, then the inferior
party envies and hates the superior, and the powerful
disdains and insults the weaker. Thus, the one being vexed

14

by his inferiority, the other puffed up with his gains, they turn from their former friendship to disagreements and wars. Under the impact of some such reasoning Pompey began to arm himself against Caesar. And as he thought he could not easily overthrow him by himself, he formed an even tighter bond with Crassus, so that he might accomplish it with his assistance. They agreed they could not hope to achieve anything as private citizens, but if they held the consulship they would be a counterweight to Caesar in managing public affairs, and they expected they could then quickly get the best of him, being two against one.

In April of 56 B.C. the triumvirs met at Luca, the southernmost town in Caesar's Cisalpine province, and patched up their alliance. Caesar agreed to support Pompey and Crassus for the consulship of the following year, they in turn to enact a five-year extension of his command in Gaul. The uneasy balance persisted till 53 B.C., when Crassus' death (in an abortive invasion of Parthia) left a situation that quickly became increasingly polarized between the two remaining protagonists. "Pompey could brook no equal, Caesar no superior."

Cicero, *Correspondence with Friends,* Book 1, no. 7
[Rome, late August 56 B.C.]
Marcus Tullius Cicero sends greetings to Publius Lentulus, proconsul [of Cilicia].
 . . . You write that you want to know about the political situation. Well, there is the most violent dissension, but the sides are not equally matched. They who are stronger in resources, arms and power in general, seem to me to have progressed, thanks to the stupidity and wavering on our side, so far as to have the advantage now in influence as well. Thus they have obtained from the senate, with very few voting nay, everything they hardly thought they could have gotten from the people without an uproar: Caesar has been voted pay for his troops and allowed ten lieutenants, and has easily arranged not to be superseded in his province. . . .

At the time of this and the following letters Cicero's brother Quintus was a legate on Caesar's staff in Gaul.

Cicero, *Letters to his Brother Quintus,* Book 2, no. 16 [15 in some editions]

[Rome, September 54 B.C.]

. . . I come now to what should perhaps have come first. What welcome news you send regarding Britain. I was afraid of the ocean, I was afraid of the island's coast — not that I make light of the other difficulties, but those raise more hope than fear, and I was uneasy at the suspense rather than actually alarmed. But you, I see, have an exceptional *matière* to write about: topography, description of places and things, customs, peoples, battles, and the kind of general you have. . . . But tell me, dear brother, what does Caesar really think of my poem?[15] He wrote me before this that he had read the first book, and he said that even in Greek he had never read anything better than the first part but found the rest to a certain degree *plutôt négligé* (that's the expression he used). Tell me the truth, is it the subject or the *genre* he doesn't like? You needn't be afraid, I'll still think not a whit less of myself.

The consuls are anxious to hold the elections, but the accused [candidates] are against it, especially Memmius because he hopes that with Caesar's arrival [in Cisalpine Gaul for the winter] he will be made consul. . . .

Ibid. Book 3, no. 1

[Rome, 28 September 54 B.C.]

. . . I come now to your letters which I received in several batches when I was at Arpinum — three, apparently dispatched by you at the same time, arrived in one day. . . . You write that Caesar has the greatest affection for me. You should encourage that, and I will do everything I can to enhance it. Regarding Pompey I am watching my step and will do as you advise. . . .

Your remark that you are becoming a greater favorite with Caesar every day gives me undying joy, and Balbus, for helping along in that direction (as you write), is the apple of my eye. . . . It is great good news you tell that he will soon be coming to Rome "loaded" and will stay with me right through to next May 15th. . . .

Just as I was folding up this letter, messengers arrived from you and Caesar — on September 21st, their twenty-seventh day on the road. . . . I certainly can have no "second thoughts"[16] where Caesar is concerned: with me he comes second only to you and our children, and a close second. That is, I think, my considered judgment, and with good cause, but I am no doubt also influenced by warm personal regard. . . .

Cicero, *Letters to Atticus,* Book 4, no. 16 [17 in some editions]
[Rome, 1 October 54 B.C.]
. . . Now to the rest of the news. According to my brother's letters Caesar has given certain manifestations of affection for me, and hard as they are to believe they are confirmed by a most fulsome letter from Caesar himself. There is an uneasy wait for the outcome of the war in Britain, as it has been determined that the approaches to the island are protected by amazing cliffs. It has also been ascertained that there is not a scrap of silver in that island, and no hope of any booty except slaves. . . .

Cicero, *Letters to his Brother Quintus,* Book 3, no. 2
[Rome, 11 October 54 B.C.]
. . . The fellow's in a tight fix unless our darling Pompey upsets the applecart, against the wishes of gods and men. . . .

All the candidates for consul have been indicted for bribery: Domitius Calvinus by [the tribune] Memmius, [the other] Memmius by Quintus Acutius, a fine upstanding young lawyer, Messala by Quintus Pompeius, and Scaurus by Triarius. There is a great hubbub over the affair, because it's plainly curtains for one or the other, these men or the laws. Pressures are being exerted against holding the trials. It looks like we're headed toward an *interregnum.*

Plutarch, *Life of Caesar,* chapter 28 [in part]
Caesar had long since decided on Pompey's overthrow, just as the latter had on his. Crassus had been keeping his eye on both of them; but now that he had perished in Parthia, it remained for the one [Caesar] wanting to become the greatest to overthrow the one [Pompey] who actually

was, or for the latter, if he would avoid such fate, to act first to eliminate the one he feared. Only recently had this fear made itself felt to Pompey, who had previously disdained Caesar, thinking it would be no great effort for him to overthrow a man he himself had elevated. Caesar, on the other hand, had from the start fashioned the following master-plan: he removed himself, like an athlete, far from his rivals and, by exercising himself in the Gallic wars, he trained his soldiery and enhanced his reputation, as his achievements rivaled the successes of Pompey.

Inscriptiones Latinae Selectae, no. 877

At Auximum in Picenum, Pompey's home territory, on the base of a statue erected to celebrate his sole consulship, 52 B.C.:

To Gnaeus Pompeius Magnus, imperator, thrice consul, our patron. [Erected] at public expense.

Dio Cassius, *Roman History*, Book 40, chapters 58-60 [selections]

[52 B.C.] Cato did not really want any office. But he saw Caesar and Pompey outgrowing the constitution, and he suspected that they would either exercise control of the state together or would quarrel with each other and engage in a very big civil war, with the victor emerging as sole ruler. Wanting to overthrow them before they engaged in active hostilities, he stood for the consulship to use against them, since as a private citizen he would have no power. But their supporters guessed that he would do something of the sort, and he was rejected at the polls. Instead, Marcus Marcellus and Sulpicius Rufus were elected, the one for his legal expertise, the other for his effectiveness as a speaker. . . .

[51 B.C.] Pompey pretended that he too disapproved of Caesar's being relieved of his command [in Gaul] prematurely, but he worked it so that when Caesar had completed the time granted him, which was not far off but due to happen the very next year, he would have to lay down his arms and return home to the life of a private citizen. . . .

[50 B.C.] After exercising so important a command for such a long period, Caesar was not about to become a private citizen again and thus put himself in his enemies'

18

hands. Instead, he made preparations to remain in office despite them: he enrolled additional soldiers, collected a war chest, forged arms, and governed in a manner to please all.

Cicero, *Correspondence with Friends,* Book 8, no. 14 [in part]

[Rome, ca. 5 August 50 B.C.]

Caelius to Cicero, greeting.

. . . On the political situation in general, as I have written you repeatedly I see no peace a year from now, and the nearer that inevitable clash approaches the more clearly its dangers appear. The issue over which our potentates are going to fight is this: Gnaeus Pompey is resolved not to allow Gaius Caesar to become consul unless he first hands over his army and provinces, but Caesar, persuaded there is no safety for him if he is separated from his army, offers the following compromise — that they both give up their armies. Thus their great friendship and their abominable alliance have not merely degenerated into behind-the-scenes recriminations, but have erupted into war.

I can't figure out what course of action it would best serve my own interests to pursue, and I doubt not but you are agonizing over the same problem. I have ties of favor and family with the one side, and I hate some members of the other cause. I am sure you are not unaware that in domestic discord men ought to follow the more honorable party as long as the struggle is carried on by legal means, not military; but when it comes to war and pitched battles one should choose the stronger side, satisfied that it is better because it is safer. In the present conflict I see the senate and solid citizens siding with Pompey, while all who live in fear and despair will flock to Caesar because his army is beyond compare. May we but have time enough to weigh the resources of each and choose our side! . . .

To sum up: You ask what I think will happen. Unless one or other of them goes off to a Parthian war, I see the threat of great conflict, to be settled by force and the sword. Both are ready in spirit and might. If it could only happen without extreme danger [to us], how you might enjoy the great spectacle that Fate is preparing!

4

The Final Break

Dio Cassius, *Roman History*, Book 41, chapters 1-4
[49 B.C.] On the very first day of the month on which
Cornelius Lentulus and Gaius Claudius entered upon their
consulate, Curio came to Rome bringing a letter from Caesar
addressed to the senate, but he did not deliver it to the
consuls until they arrived at the senate-house, for fear that
if they received it outside they might suppress it. As it was
they held back a long time, reluctant to read it out; but in
the end they were compelled by the tribunes Quintus Cassius Longinus and Mark Antony to make it public. Antony,
for the service he there rendered Caesar, was destined to
be abundantly repaid by advancement to high office.

In the letter Caesar detailed all the benefits he had conferred upon the commonwealth, and he rebutted the charges
brought against him. He promised to disband his army
and relinquish his office if Pompey did the same, but as
long as the latter retained his arms it was not right to com-
pel him to disarm, thus delivering him into the hands of
his enemies. When the vote on this proposal was taken —
not by roll call, where they might be shamed or frightened
into voting against their consciences, but by a division of
the house — no one voted that Pompey should surrender
his arms (for his forces were stationed in the suburbs), but
all except Marcus Caelius and the Curio who had brought
the letter voted for Caesar to do so. . . .

This, then, was the decision, but Antony and Longinus
did not allow any part of it to be ratified either on that day
or on the next. The others, in exasperation voted to change
to mourning garb, but this too was vetoed by the same

men. Nevertheless the resolution was recorded in the minutes and put into effect; all immediately left the senate-house, changed their robes, and returned to debate the question of punishment for the tribunes. On seeing this the tribunes at first fought back, but then they took fright, especially when [the consul] Lentulus advised them to clear off before the vote was taken. After much talk and protestation they took off with Curio and Caelius to go to Caesar, little bothered by their expulsion from the senate. The senators then passed the resolution entrusting the protection of the city to the consuls and the other magistrates, as was the custom [for martial law]. Next they went outside the pomerium to Pompey himself, declared a state of emergency, and turned over to him both money and troops. They also voted that Caesar hand over his command to his successor and disband his legions by a certain day or be proclaimed an enemy acting contrary to the interests of the fatherland.

When Caesar learned of these happenings he came to Ariminum,[17] advancing for the first time outside the area of his command. There he assembled his troops and had Curio and the others with him relate what had taken place. When they had finished he himself spoke to the occasion, spurring them further. After that he set out and marched straight for Rome itself, winning over all the cities en route without a fight: in some the garrisons fled because of their weakness, in others they voluntarily went over to his side. Observing this, and learning all Caesar's plans from Labienus, who had abandoned and deserted Caesar and was betraying all his secrets, Pompey took fright. . . .

Suetonius, *Life of the Deified Julius Caesar*, chapters 31-32

[49 B.C.] When he received word that the tribunes' veto had been nullified and they themselves forced to flee the city, he immediately sent some cohorts ahead — secretly, so as not to arouse suspicion — but himself made a pretense of attending public games, examining the plans for a gladiatorial school he was going to build,[18] and dining as usual with a large company. Then, after sunset, he took mules from a nearby bakery, harnessed them to a carriage, and set out very secretly with a small escort. His lights went out, he lost his way and roamed about for a considerable time, but at last, toward dawn, he found a guide and got out by following very narrow trails on foot. He rejoined his cohorts at the Rubicon river, which was the boundary of his province. There he paused a while, thinking over the magnitude of his undertaking. Turning to his retinue he said, "Even now we can still retreat. But once we cross this little bridge, everything will have to be settled by arms."

As he hesitated the following sign appeared. All at once a figure of exceptional size and beauty appeared, seated hard by and playing on a pipe. There gathered round to hear him not only shepherds but also a sizable number of soldiers from their posts, among them some trumpeters. Then he took a trumpet from one of them, rushed to the river, sounded the war call with a mighty blast, and crossed to the opposite bank. Thereupon Caesar said, "Let our march go whither the signs of the gods and the iniquity of our enemies call. The die is cast."[19]

Plutarch, *Life of Caesar*, chapter 32

Caesar had with him not more than 300 horse and 5,000 foot. The rest of his men had been left behind, beyond the Alps, and officers were sent to bring them too. But for now, for the start and first step of his enterprise, he needed, he saw, not so much a large force as boldness and lightning speed in seizing the opportunity: attacking with his whole force would be less effective than spreading consternation by doing the unexpected. He therefore ordered his centurions and other officers to go with just their swords, leaving their other weapons, and seize Ariminum, a large city of [Cisalpine] Gaul with as little bloodshed and disturbance as possible. . . .

He himself spent the day in public, attending and watching a workout of gladiators. Shortly before evening he performed his toilet, then went into the dining hall and socialized a while with the invitees to supper. Then, as dusk was coming on, he rose to go, asking the company to be good enough to await his return. A few of his friends, however, had been given instructions to follow him, not all together but one this way and another that way. He himself mounted one of the hired vehicles and drove first along another road, then turned toward Ariminum. When he came to the river Rubicon, which is the boundary between Cisalpine Gaul and the rest of Italy, he was assailed by considerations of pros and cons — the closer he approached his adventure the more he was moved by its awesome magnitude. He checked his course and ordered a halt, then mulled over and over in silence, changing his mind and back again, his resolution undergoing many fluctuations. He also reviewed the matter in detail with his friends who were present, among them Asinius Pollio, estimating what woes his crossing the river would let loose for all mankind, how great the fame of it they would leave to posterity. At last, in a sort of passion, as if releasing himself from such calculation and turning to face the future, he uttered the prefatory words commonly spoken by men plunging into uncertain and daring risks: "Let the die be cast." Then he hurried across the river and, continuing at full speed, raced into Ariminum before dawn and seized it. The night before the crossing he is said to have had a monstrous dream, in which he saw himself enjoying incestuous intercourse with his own mother.[20]

5

Civil War

Dio Cassius, *Roman History*, Book 41, chapters 5-6
Pompey judged, from the reports he received, that the
force he had mustered was no match for Caesar's. He
therefore changed his plan, the more so as he saw that the
people at Rome, and most particularly his own partisans,
remembering as they did the horrors of Marius and Sulla,
had no stomach for this war and wanted only to get out
of it safely. He accordingly sent envoys to Caesar, namely
Lucius Caesar, a relative of his, and Lucius Roscius, a
praetor, both of whom volunteered to go and ask if he
would suspend his attack and come to an agreement on
reasonable terms. Caesar in reply repeated what he had
said in his letter, adding that he was more than willing to
talk it over with Pompey. The Roman people were not
pleased at hearing this, fearing that the two generals might
come to some agreement to their disadvantage. But the
envoys were lavish in their praises of Caesar, and added
at the end of their report a promise that no one would
suffer any harm at his hands and that the legions would
be disbanded forthwith. Then they were pleased: they sent
the same envoys back to him [to conclude the negotiations],
and they were loud in their constantly repeated demand
that both of them lay down their arms simultaneously.

Pompey was frightened by this demand, knowing full
well that he would be much inferior to Caesar if they were
dependent upon the favor of the people. Consequently,
before the envoys returned he took off with his troops for
Campania, figuring he could fight there more easily. He
ordered the whole senate together with the magistrates to

follow him, decreeing immunity for their absence from Rome and proclaiming that he would regard anyone who stayed behind as the like and equal of those actively working against their party. In addition he instructed them to vote the seizure of all the public moneys and dedicatory offerings in the city, hoping this wealth would enable him to enrol great numbers of soldiers. All the cities in Italy regarded him with such favor that on hearing he was dangerously ill, a little while back, they had vowed to offer public sacrifices for his recovery. No one would deny that this was a great distinction they then conferred upon him; nothing of the sort had ever been voted anyone else. . . . But even so this offered no firm assurance that they might not abandon him out of fear of a stronger man.

Cicero, *Letters to Atticus*, Book 7, no. 11
[About the 20th of January, 49 B.C.]

Tell me, what's all this! What's going on? I'm in the dark. According to Pompey's communiqués, "We hold Cingulum, we've lost Ancona, Labienus has deserted Caesar." Are we talking about a general of the Roman people, or about a Hannibal? The wretched fool [Caesar], who has never perceived even a semblance of the *bonum et aequum*. And he says he's doing it all for honor's sake. But where is honor without morality? Is it moral to lead an army without public authorization, to seize cities inhabited by Roman citizens so as to open the way more easily to the mother city, to machinate *abolitions de dettes, rappel d'exilés*,[21] a thousand enormities,

"all to obtain the greatest of divinities, sole rule"?[22]

I wish him joy of his good fortune . . .

To come back to our friend Pompey. What, in heaven's name, do you think of his decision? I mean his abandoning Rome. *J'en suis perplexe.* The most absurd thing in the world. So you abandon Rome. I suppose you'd do the same if the Gauls were marching on the city? . . .

Still, to judge from the indignant talk I hear in the towns hereabout, Pompey's decision may have a good effect after all. There is a remarkable public outcry — in Rome too? you must let me know — at the city's being without magistrates, without senate. And lastly, Pompey's flight from

25

Rome moves people dramatically. In a word, it's become a whole other ball game. *Now* people are for making no concessions to Caesar. You explain this to me.

I'm in charge of an activity that should give me little trouble. Pompey wants me to be the *surveillant* of all this part of Campania and the coast, with authority over recruiting and general administration. So I expect I'll be moving about. I imagine you see by now the direction of Caesar's *poussée*, how the people feel, how the whole business looks. Please write me, and as often as possible since things change so fast. I feel some relief both when writing you letters and when reading yours.

Ibid., no. 12
[Formiae, 22 January 49 B.C.]
I have so far received only one letter from you, dated the 19th, in which you refer to an earlier one, which I have not yet received. But please continue writing as often as possible, not only anything you learn or hear, but even anything you may suspect — and above all what you think I ought to do or not do.

You ask me to let you know what Pompey is doing. I don't think he knows himself; certainly none of us does. I saw Lentulus, the consul, at Formiae yesterday, and I saw Libo: nothing but trepidation and disarray. Pompey is making for Larinum, where there are some cohorts, as well as at Luceria and Teanum and the rest of Apulia. From there — no one knows whether he wants to make any kind of stand or to cross the sea. If he stays, I don't see how he can have a strong army. If he goes — where to, how, what do I do? I simply don't know.

As for [Caesar], I expect him to produce nothing but atrocities. You may be sure that neither the suspension of public business nor the departure of the senate and magistrates nor the closing of the treasury will give him pause. But about that, as you write, we will soon know.

Meanwhile, please forgive me for writing you so much and so often. If affords me some relief, and besides I want to elicit letters from you, especially your advice on what I should do, how I am to conduct myself. Commit myself completely to Pompey's cause? The danger doesn't frighten

me, but I am overcome with grief at his having done everything without my advice or even contrary to my advice.
Or should I temporize and shuffle, and then align myself
with those who prevail, who gain the upper hand? *Je crains
l'opinion des Troyens.*[23] The duties of a citizen and of a friend
call me back, and yet I am often consumed with pity for
our children's future.

So write me at least, even though you must be torn by
the same worries. Above all, tell me what you think I ought
to do if Pompey leaves Italy. Manius Lepidus at least, with
whom I have talked about it, is sure it will end that way;
so does Lucius Torquatus. . . . I don't expect any guar-
antees from you, only your opinion. And I also want to
know your own *embarras*.

It seems pretty much agreed that Labienus has deserted
Caesar. If it could have happened that he came to Rome
and found magistrates and senate there, that would have
been a big boost for our cause: he would have been perceived as condemning a friend's illegality for the greater
good of the republic. As it is that's how it appears, but the
benefit is less. For there's no one [in Rome] he can help,
and I imagine he's sorry about that. Unless, of course, the
very fact of his defection is a false rumor. Here at least it
was reported as definite.

And I'd like you — even though you write that you are
sticking strictly to family matters — I'd like you to describe
to me the way things look in the city: any sign that Pompey
is missed, any resentment of Caesar? Also, what you think
about Terentia and Tullia[24] — should they stay in Rome,
or join me here, or go to some safe place? That and anything
else is what I'd like you to write, or rather keep on writing.

Ibid., no. 22

[Formiae, 9 February 49 B.C.]
As far as I can see there isn't a foot of Italian soil that isn't
in that man's power. About Pompey I know nothing, and
I think he'll be intercepted unless he takes ship. What
incredible speed! Whereas our man — well, I can't list his
faults without pain, since I am tormented with anxiety
about him.

Your fear of a massacre is surely not without foundation — not that anything would be less calculated to contribute to the long duration of Caesar's victory and rule, but I see whose advice he's going to follow. . . .

As for myself, what am I to do? How am I to follow, by land or sea, a leader whose whereabouts I don't know? In fact, by land, how can I? by sea, where to? Shall I then turn myself in to his adversary? Supposing I could do so safely — as many urge — I couldn't do so honorably, could I? By no means. Am I, then, to ask your advice, as usual? The problem is insoluble. Still, if you do get an idea, please write — also what you yourself are going to do.

Ibid., **Book 8, no. 11**
[Formiae, 27 February 49 B.C.]
You think I am confused and distraught, and so I am, but perhaps not as much as you imagine. For worry is always relieved when one's thinking reaches a decision or a dead end. I could, of course, spend whole days lamenting; but that I fear, aside from accomplishing nothing, would discredit my studies and writings. I therefore spend all my time reflecting on the powerful example of that virtuous man whom I portrayed in my books with reasonable accuracy — at least in your opinion.[25] Do you remember the ideal statesman that I proposed as a model? In the fifth book Scipio says this, as I recall: "As the pilot's goal is a successful voyage, the doctor's good health, the general's a victory, so our statesman aims to provide for the citizens a happy life, secure in resources, abounding in wealth, great in glory, honored for virtue. Such is the work, the greatest and noblest in human society, that I would have him carry out."

To this our Gnaeus [Pompey] has never given a thought, and now less than ever. For both of them the goal of their actions has been absolute rule, not a happy and honorable commonwealth. Pompey did not abandon Rome because he could not defend it, Italy because he was driven from it. From the first he planned to turn the world upside down, to stir up foreign kings, to bring savage peoples under arms into Italy, to organize huge armies. His appetite has long been for Sulla's kind of rule, and many of his associates desire it. And don't think Pompey and Caesar couldn't yet come to some agreement, some understanding. Even now it's possible. But neither has our happiness as his *objectif*. Both want to reign.

There, you wanted me to give you my views on our troubles, and I have answered you in a few words. *En prophète*, my dear Atticus, not divining like poor Cassandra whom nobody believed but guessing . . . I can vaticinate: a veritable Iliad of woes impends, worse for us who remain at home than for them who have crossed the sea with Pompey, because while they have only one of the the two to fear, we have both.[26] Why, then, have I stayed, you will ask. Perhaps at your advice, perhaps because I didn't meet up with Pompey, perhaps because it was the more moral course. But I tell you, this summer you will see unhappy Italy trampled under foot by the fearsome armies of both, recruited from every kind of riffraff. And the frightful outlook is not so much for pillage as for total destruction — so great will be, as I see it, the two forces in conflict. Perhaps you have been expecting some consolation [from me]? I can't find any. Nothing can be more wretched, more desperate, more foul.

You ask what Caesar has written me. The same as before: he's very glad I've stayed out of it, and he prays I will continue to do so . . .[27]

I have received two letters from Pompey. I enclose copies, because I'd like you to observe how ridiculous they are, how meticulous my replies.

I'm waiting to hear the results of Caesar's dash across Apulia to Brundisium . . . As soon as I hear anything I'll write you. I'd like you to write me what responsible people are saying. Rome is full of them, I hear. Yes I know, you don't make public appearances, but even so you can't help hearing a lot.

Ibid., no. 13
[Formiae, 1 March 49 B.C.]
The eye inflammation is still with me, hence this letter in my secretary's handwriting and also its brevity — although for now at least I really have no news. Everything now depends on the news from Brundisium. If Caesar has caught up with our friend Gnaeus, there is still a flickering hope

for peace, but if Pompey has already crossed over, I fear it means war to the death.

But just look at the kind of man [Caesar] into whose hands the republic has fallen: clearsighted, alert, on the ball. Bless me, if he doesn't kill anyone and doesn't confiscate anyone's property he will be most worshipped by the very people who most dreaded him. The townspeople and farmers hereabouts talk to me a lot, and it's clear they care about nothing but their land, their simple abodes and their money. And see, too, how the situation has been reversed: the man they used to trust they now fear, and the one they used to fear they now adore. I cannot reflect without distress on the extent to which our mistakes and faults are responsible for this outcome.

Well, I've written you what I think impends, and now I await a letter from you.

Ibid., no. 16
[Formiae, 4 March 49 B.C.]
All my arrangements are made except for a safe and secret route across the Adriatic. (I can't face going by the Tyrrhenian sea at this time of year.) By what route am I to come to the place to which my mind is made up and the state of affairs calls me? I must leave here quickly or I may be stopped or detained. What makes me go now is not, as one might think, Pompey. I have long known him to be *comme politique le pire* of men, and now I see he is also *le pire des stratégistes*.

So my reason for going is not Pompey but what, as I learn from Philotimus' letters, people are saying about me. He says the optimates are ripping me up the back. What optimates, by god! See how they now rush to welcome Caesar, and how they are ingratiating themselves with him! The country towns worship him as a very god, and they're not just going through the motions, as they did in offering prayers when Pompey was ailing. . . . Can you imagine the *cris d'accueil* from the towns, the honors they shower upon him! From fear, you will say. No doubt, but for a fact they are even more frightened of his opponent. They are enthralled by Caesar's insidious clemency, and terrified of Pompey's rages. . . .

30

So I have no illusions about the prospect as I set out to join a man readier to devastate Italy than to defeat his enemy, and I am prepared for a tyrant. As I write this, on the 4th, I am expecting some word from Brundisium any minute. But why do I say "some" word? The news will tell of how disgracefully he fled [across the Adriatic], and by what route and when the victor will make his way to these parts. When I learn that, if he comes by the Appian Way I think I'll go to Arpinum.

Ibid., **Book 9, no. 16**
[Formiae, 26 march 49 B.C.]
Although I have nothing to write you, still I send you this so as not to miss a day. It is reported that Caesar will stop at Sinuessa tomorrow. I have been handed a letter from him dated today, in which he looks forward to my cooperative "efforts," not just "effort" as in his previous letter. Here is today's letter, written in reply to mine praising him for his notable clemency at Corfinium:

> Caesar Imperator to Cicero Imperator, greeting.
> You surmise correctly — for you know me well — that nothing is further from my nature than cruelty. And while I certainly take great pleasure in that fact, I am proud and happy that my action meets with your approval. And it does not bother me to learn that the men I let go free have gone off to make war on me again. I want nothing more than for me to be true to myself and them to their selves. But you, I should like you to attend me in town so that I may as usual have the benefit of your counsels and efforts in all matters. . . .

Dio Cassius, *Roman History*, **Book 41, chapters 9-13**
So Pompey abandoned Rome, taking some of the senators with him; others, either sympathizing with Caesar's cause or remaining neutral, stayed behind. He hurriedly raised troops from the cities, collected funds, and sent a garrison to every strategic point. When Caesar learned of this, he did not hasten to Rome, since he knew it was the prize awaiting those who would win, and moreover he claimed to be marching not against it because it was hostile to him,

but against his political adversaries so as to protect it. He sent letters throughout Italy challenging Pompey to some kind of trial of strength, and bidding all others to have no fear, to stay where they were, and making them many promises. Then making a dash for Corfinium, which was held by Lucius Domitius and would not come over to him, he defeated in battle some he encountered on the way, and shut up the rest under siege.

Pompey, then, with these besieged and many of his other supporters defecting to Caesar, had no further hope of controlling Italy and decided to cross the sea to Macedonia, Greece and Asia. The memory of his great accomplishments there, and the friendship of peoples and kings, offered great encouragement. Spain, too, was all for him, but he could not get there safely with Caesar in control of both [Cis- and Transalpine] Gauls. Furthermore, he calculated that if he sailed away no one would pursue him, owing to an insufficiency of ships and the onset of winter. Meanwhile he would have time to collect lots of money and troops from subjects and allies. With that intention he set out for Brundisium, and he sent orders to Domitius to abandon Corfinium and go with him. . . . But as Domitius was making preparations for a safe evacuation, his staff, learning of it and refusing to take part in a departure that was really a rout, went over to Caesar. So they joined his army, while Domitius and the others, after being rebuked by Caesar for arraying themselves against him, were allowed safe passage and went off to Pompey.

Now Caesar was in a hurry to close with Pompey before he could sail away, in other words, to fight it out with him by overtaking him while he was still in Italy . . . But seeing how hard it would be to capture Brundisium, he offered him an agreement restoring peace and friendship between them. Pompey replied only that he would communicate Caesar's offer to the consuls. But as they had already decided to parley with no citizen who was under arms, Caesar threw his army against the city. Pompey repelled him for a few days, till the ships returned. Then he blocked and barricaded the streets leading to the harbor, so no one could attack during his embarcation, and he put out by night. He crossed safely to Macedonia, but Brundisium was captured and in it two ships filled with his men.

Thus Pompey abandoned both Rome and the rest of Italy, choosing to carry out the exact opposite of his earlier course, when he had sailed home from Asia. And his resulting fame and fortune were also the opposite . . . Instead of arriving with the brilliant reputation gained in those earlier wars, he now sailed off covered with humiliation because of his fear of Caesar. And instead of the glory he had gained for making his country more powerful, he now became most inglorious for deserting her.

Cicero, *Correspondence with Friends*, Book 9, no. 9

From Caesar's camp in Epirus [and probably at Caesar's request]

Dolabella writes to Cicero, his father-in-law, who was now with Pompey. The time is May of 48 B.C., a month or less before the decisive battle at Pharsalus.

If you are well, I rejoice. I too am well, and our Tullia is in splendid health. Terentia was not so well, but I know for a fact that she is now fully recovered.[28] Everything else is just fine at your house.

In the past there was never any reason for you to think that it was out of partisanship rather than in your own interest that I kept urging you either to join us on Caesar's side or at least retire into neutrality. So now that the scales have tipped toward our victory I surely cannot be viewed as doing other than offering you such suasion as, in filial duty bound, I could not leave unsaid. And you, my dear Cicero, please receive my words, whether they meet with your approval or not, in the assurance that they are pondered and written with the best of intentions and in a spirit of complete devotion to you.

You observe that Gnaeus Pompey has been saved neither by the glamor of his name and achievements, nor by his patronage of kings and nations that he never stopped boasting about. He cannot even obtain what the lowliest of men can, for he cannot even escape with honor, driven as he is from Italy, with both Spains lost to him, his veteran army captured and he himself now beleaguered (I doubt that has ever happened before to a Roman imperator).

33

Therefore consider with your usual acumen what he or you can hope for. In that way you will most easily adopt the policy that will be most useful to you . . . You have already satisfied the claims of duty and friendship, you have also satisfied those of party and of the form of government you favored. The only thing to do is to accept the republic as it now is, rather than pursue the old and end up with none.

Therefore, my most amiable Cicero, if Pompey should be driven from hereabouts as well and should be forced again to depart for other regions, please betake yourself to Athens or to some other city uninvolved in the war. If you will do that, please write me [where you will be], so that I may fly to your side if at all possible.

As for anything regarding your political eminence [in the future], that will have to be obtained from our victorious general.[29] Caesar is a man of such kindness that it will be the easiest thing in the world for you to obtain it from him yourself, and I think my entreaties will have no small influence with him. And in keeping with your own good faith and kindness, please see to it that the messenger with whom I send you this is allowed to return to me and brings me a letter from you.

The Battle of Pharsalus, 48 B.C.
Dio Cassius, *Roman History* Book 41, chapters 52-63 [selections]

Pompey, then, was once again becoming powerful. He did then not pursue Caesar, who had made a hasty retreat by night across the Genusus river; he was fully convinced that the war was over. Accordingly, he took the title of *imperator*. . .

After this Pompey set out after Caesar and came into Thessaly. As they lay opposite each other the appearance of the camps bore some semblance of war, but the weapons lay idle, just as in time of peace. As they considered the size of the stakes, looked ahead to an unclear and uncertain outcome, and still felt some qualms because of their common origin and kinship, they continued to delay. In this interval they even exchanged offers of friendship, and some even thought they would come to an agreement. But it would have been an empty one, for the reason that they were both striving for supreme power, driven by great innate ambition and great acquired rivalry. Men can least endure to be inferior to their equals and closest associates. These two, therefore, both thinking they had the power to be victorious, were unwilling to make any concession to each other, or to trust that, if they did come to some agreement, they could possibly avoid exerting themselves to come out on top, thus falling out again over the supremacy. In their purposes they differed from each other to this extent, that Pompey had his heart set on being second to no man, Caesar on being first of all; the former's efforts were aimed at being held in honor by willing people, to rule and be loved without compulsion, but to the latter it mattered not at all if he ruled even unwilling people, commanded men who hated him, bestowed his honors upon himself. But in their actions, by which they expected to accomplish all their desires, they were perforce both alike. It was impossible for anyone to attain such ends without making war on his countrymen, leading foreigners against kindred, unjustly pillaging large quantities of money, and lawlessly killing one's dearest friends. Hence, even though they differed in their desires, nevertheless in their acts, by which they expected to fulfill those desires, they were alike. And that is why, despite their many protestations, they would yield nothing to each other and in the end came to blows.

The contest was great and like no other. The leaders themselves were reputed to be in all matters of warfare the best and clearly the most renowned, not only of the Romans but even of all other men then living. They had been trained in military matters since boyhood, had always been engaged in them, had performed notable deeds, had displayed great bravery and enjoyed great good fortune, were most worthy of being generals, most worthy of being victorious. . . .

Such was the contest in which they were joined. But they did not close immediately: originating from the same fatherland and the same hearth, having practically the same weapons and military formations, they shrank from beginning the battle, they shrank from killing one another, and there was prolonged silence and dejection on both sides. No one advanced or moved at all, but all stood bowed and motionless, as if dead. Finally Caesar and Pompey, fearing that if they remained quiet any longer their ardor might be dulled or they might even come to terms, snapped orders for the trumpeters to sound and for the men to join in raising the war cry. This was done on both sides, but they were far from being filled with martial spirit: the trumpets sounding the same note and themselves shouting in the same language revealed anew their common origin and reemphasized their kinship. As a result, they fell to weeping and lamenting. But at length the contingents of allied troops went ahead and started things, and then the Romans joined in, aghast at themselves. Those who fought from a distance were less aware of the horror — they used their bows, javelins and slings without knowing whom they hit. But the infantry and cavalry got the worst of it, because they were in close combat and could even exchange a few words. They would recognize those lined up against them at the very moment of wounding them, call them by name as they killed them, remember their native cities as they despoiled them. Wherever they met each other this is what the Romans and their Italian allies did and suffered. . . .

For a very long time their struggle was evenly balanced. But in the end, after many on both sides alike had fallen or been wounded, Pompey, the greater part of whose army was Asiatic and untrained, was defeated. This had more or less been forecast in advance, for thunderbolts had fallen in his camp, a fire had appeared in the sky above Ceasar's encampment and then descended upon his own, bees had swarmed about his military standards, and many of his sacrificial victims had escaped while being led to the altars. And the reverberations of this great battle were felt on the very same day by the rest of mankind. The clash of arms and armies occurred in many places. In Pergamum a sound of drums and cymbals arose from the temple of Dionysus and spread through the whole city. In Tralles a palm tree sprang up in the shrine of Victory, and the goddess herself turned to face a bust of Caesar by her side. In Syria two young men announced the outcome of the battle and vanished. At Padua, which is now part of Italy but then still belonged to [Cisalpine] Gaul, some birds not only flew in with the news but in a way acted it out, so that a man named Gaius Cornelius accurately inferred from their behavior all that had happened and recounted it to the bystanders. As each of these things occurred on that very same day they were at first disbelieved, as might be expected, but they were long marveled at after the official reports of the events arrived.

The survivors of the Pompeians fled every which way or surrendered. Those of them who were soldiers of the line Caesar enrolled in his own legions, and he bore them no ill will. But of the senators and equites he put to death those whom he had previously captured and spared (but he did except a few whom his friends begged off, allowing them on this occasion to save one each); the rest — those who had then fought against him for the first time — he set free, saying, "In no way have I been wronged by anyone who supported the cause of Pompey out of friendship and received no benefaction from me." He acted in the same way toward the princes and peoples that had joined Pompey: he pardoned them all, taking into consideration that he himself knew few if any of them, whereas they had in the past received many benefactions from Pompey. In fact he praised these in contrast to those who had benefited from but then deserted Pompey in the recent dangers; he could hope the former kind would be favorably disposed to himself, but the latter, he reckoned, being betrayers of their current friend, would not spare him either at some future time, no matter how eager they now seemed to do anything to gratify him. . . . Such clemency and goodness did he show to all who had fought against him. In fact, the letters stored in Pompey's chests that might give evidence of various individuals' favoring Pompey or disfavoring himself he refused even to read or have copied, but he burned them at once so as not to be compelled by their contents to do anything drastic. That is still another reason to despise the men who conspired against him. I say this particularly because Marcus Brutus Caepio, who later slew him, was here captured and spared by him.

37

II

THE VICTIM

From Pharsalus to the Ides of March
[48-44 BC]

. . . no small or ordinary crime.
— Appian, *Civil Wars* iv.17.134

. . . as he was ambitious, I slew him.
— Shakespeare, *Julius Caesar* ii.2

We shall be called purgers, not murderers.
— *ibid*. ii.1

6

The Aftermath of Pharsalus

**Caesar, *The Civil War*, Book 3,
chapters 102-106**

Caesar decided to drop everything and pursue Pompey wherever he had fled to, in that way preventing him from collecting another army and renewing the war. He advanced every day as far as he could on horseback, while one legion was ordered to follow by shorter marches. An edict had been posted at Amphipolis in Pompey's name ordering all the young men of the province, Greeks and Roman citizens alike, to report for swearing in. But it was unclear whether Pompey had done that in order to disarm suspicion and hide for as long as possible his true plan of a more distant flight, or because he really intended, if allowed time, to raise new troops and try to hold Macedonia. Pompey stopped one night at anchor at Amphipolis, conferred with his friends there and collected money for necessary expenses, but when he was informed that Caesar was approaching he took off and a few days later arrived at Mytilene.

Detained there for two days by bad weather, he acquired additional light craft and then continued on to Cilicia and Cyprus. There he learned that the people of Antioch and the Roman businessmen there had agreed to resort to arms in order to keep him out. . . . The same thing happened at Rhodes to Lucius Lentulus, a consul of the year before, and Publius Lentulus, a consular, and some others who were following Pompey in flight: when they came to the island they were not admitted to the town or even the harbor, but were notified to leave, which they did against their will. But by now news of Caesar's approach was reaching these cities.

On learning of these developments Pompey gave up his plan of going to Syria, took money from the tax-farmers' corporation and some private citizens in Cyprus, and with a great load of money for military purposes and 2,000 armed men on board . . . arrived at Pelusium [in Egypt]. There as it happened King Ptolemy, a mere boy, backed by a large force was waging war against his sister Cleopatra, whom he had driven from the throne a few months before with the aid of relatives and friends. . . . Pompey sent word to him, asking — in the name of the hospitality and friendship he had shown the king's father — for asylum in Alexandria and the king's protection in his time of need. . . . But the king's friends, who because of his youth were acting as regents, formed a secret plot. It is unclear whether they did so out of fear, as they later professed, that Pompey might corrupt the royal army and seize Alexandria and Egypt, or because they despised him in his downfall, as it often happens that in misfortune friends turn into enemies. Whatever their motivation, overtly they answered Pompey's messengers graciously, bidding him come to the king, but privately they sent Achillas, a royal officer, and Lucius Septimius, a military tribune, to assassinate Pompey. Being greeted by them courteously and reassured by the presence of Septimius, who had been a centurion under him in the pirate war, Pompey steps into their launch with a few of his men, and there he is killed by Achillas and Septimius. Similarly, Lucius Lentulus is arrested by the king and slain in prison . . .

Caesar stopped in [the Roman province of] Asia a few days. There he heard that Pompey had been seen in Cyprus, from which he guessed that he was making for Egypt, a place with which he had ties and which afforded other advantages. Accordingly Caesar went to Alexandria with the one legion that he had ordered to follow him from Thessaly and a second which he had summoned from his lieutenant Quintus Fufius in Greece, plus 800 cavalry and ten warships from Rhodes and some from Asia. The legions' strength was down to a mere 3,200 men, the rest having been invalided out by wounds and the rigor of the

41

very long marches. But Caesar did not hesitate to advance even with weak forces, confident that the report of his exploits would make him equally safe anywhere. At Alexandria he learns of the death of Pompey.

Dio Cassius, *Roman History*, Book 42, chapters 17-20

While these events were occurring abroad, at Rome, as long as the Caesar-Pompey issue was unsettled and up in the air, everybody ostensibly favored Caesar, seeing that his co-consul Servilius was right in their midst with an armed contingent. At any report of a victory there was open rejoicing, at defeat grief; in either event, while some were sincere, the rest pretended, for there were many spies and eavesdroppers prowling about, observing everything that was said and done in reaction to the news. But those who loathed Caesar and preferred Pompey's cause — what they said and did in private was the exact opposite of the public pretenses. . . .

When word was first brought of the battle of Pharsalus, people refused for a long time to credit it because Caesar sent no official dispatch (he did not want to appear to be rejoicing over such a victory, and for the same reason he celebrated no triumph for it). The pro-Pompeians, moreover, regarded the report as very unlikely, considering the relative strengths of the contestants and their own hopes. But when at last they had to believe it, they removed the busts of Pompey and Sulla from the rostra, but did nothing further for the time being. Many did not want to do even this, and many, fearing that Pompey might rise to fight again, figured that this was enough for Caesar and expected they could easily explain it away to Pompey. . . .

But when Pompey was dead, they now openly hailed the one and reviled the other, and they proposed every conceivable honor to be bestowed upon Caesar. In this there was great competition among practically all the leading men as they strove to outdo one another in flattering proposals and in voting them. With huzzas and gestures they all, as if Caesar were present and looking on, manifested the very greatest zeal, and they thought that in return for what they were doing — as if they were doing it just to gratify him and not perforce — they would immediately be rewarded with an office, a priesthood, or even money. All those other honors which had previously been voted also to others — statues, crowns, front seating, and suchlike — or which were new and then proposed for the first time but not approved by Caesar, I shall omit, for I should become tiresome if I should list them all. And I shall do the same hereafter, the more so as the proposals became ever more numerous and more absurd. I shall tell only those that were special or exceptional, and received Caesar's approval.

They granted him the right to do whatever he wanted with those who had backed Pompey's cause — not that he had not already taken that right on his own authority, but in order that he might appear to be acting under some statute. On the pretext of the Pompeian remnant in Africa they designated him arbiter of war and peace everywhere in the world, without the necessity of consulting the people or senate. This too, of course, lay in his power before, since he maintained such a large force and had fought practically all his previous wars on his own personal decision. Nevertheless, wishing to preserve the appearance of an independent citizenry, they voted him these rights and all the others that he could have had even against their will. He received the right to be consul for five years in a row, and to be chosen dictator not for six months but for a whole year. In addition he took the tribunician power practically for life, thus obtaining the right to sit on the same benches with them and — an unprecedented right — to be counted with them in all other respects. All elections of magistrates, excepting those of the plebs, were now at his discretion, and for this reason they were postponed pending his arrival and were held toward the end of the year.

Dio Cassius, *Roman History*, Book 43, chapter 14

[46 B.C.] [After his defeat of the Pompeians in Africa] Caesar returned to Rome, priding himself most especially on the brilliance of his feats but also on the senate's decrees. In honor of his victory they decreed forty days of sacrifices, and granted him the distinction of riding in his triumph (voted him earlier) drawn by white horses and accompanied by all the lictors who were then with him, plus as many more as he had had in his first dictatorship, plus as many again as he had had in his second. They chose him overseer of everyone's morals (creating some such title for him, as if that of *censor* were not good enough) for three years, and dictator for the next ten years. In addition, they voted that he should sit in the senate on a curule chair next to the successive consuls and should always be the first to express his view, that he should give the starting signal at all Circus games, and that he should designate the holders of the magistracies and other offices that the people formerly assigned. They ordered that one of his chariots be placed on the Capitol facing that of Jupiter; that a bronze statue of him, with an inscription saying that he was a demigod, be mounted on a map of the world; and that his name be inscribed on the Capitol in place of Catulus', on the ground that he had completed the temple (he had tried [sixteen years before] to call Catulus to an accounting of the costs of its construction). I have listed only these honors, not because they were the only ones voted (actually, a host of measures was introduced and of course passed), but because he declined the others but accepted these.

Cicero, *Correspondence with Friends*, Book 6, no. 6
Aulus Caecina, to whom this letter is addressed, was the son of the Caecina whose case Cicero conducted [in 65 B.C.] with a speech that is extant. The son fought on Pompey's side, and was spared by Caesar but not permitted to return to Italy. As this letter shows, he and his friends were still hoping that that ban would soon be lifted.

[Rome, late September of 46 B.C.]
Cicero to Aulus Caecina, greeting.
    . . . There are many who can attest that I warned Pompey at the start not to join up with Caesar, and later not to break with him. I saw that the senate's power would be broken by their coalition, that civil war would arise from their division. Also, I was on the most intimate terms with Caesar and thought very highly of Pompey, and my advice was at once loyal to Pompey and beneficial to both. . . .
    Their dispute erupted into war. Regarding — as I did

44

— even the most unjust peace as preferable to the most just war, what warning or remonstrance did I fail to utter? My counsel was overruled, not so much by Pompey (he in fact was impressed by it), but by those who had confidence in Pompey's generalship and thought a victory in that war would be most advantageous for their private interests and their greed. The war began, I remained on the sidelines. It was driven from Italy, I remained — as long as I could. But honor weighed more with me than fear. . . . And so I set forth. And in that war no setback occurred that I did not predict. . . .

Well then, the augury I now give you does not derive from the flight of a winged creature, nor from the sound made by a divining-bird on the left (as in our augural system), nor from the rattle of the sacred chicken feed. No, I have other signs to look for, and if not more infallible than those they are at any rate less obscure or misleading. The signs I take note of for my predictions follow, as it were, a twofold method: in one I make my deductions from Caesar himself, in the other from the nature and rationale of the political situation. In Caesar I find, first of all, a mild and merciful nature — as is portrayed in your brilliant book *Remonstrances*. Then there is the fact that outstanding intellectual gifts, such as yours, appeal to him. In addition, he is relenting at the urgings of your many friends — urgings which, he must realize, are reasonable and inspired by a sense of duty, not by baseless self-seeking. . . .

Why, then, has all this had little or no effect? Because he thinks he can not resist the appeals of many others if he accedes to you, with whom, as he sees it, he has juster cause for being angry. "What hope, then, is there for me," you will ask, "from an angry man?" He knows . . . being a man of great acumen and much foresight, that you, given your character and family ties, cannot be excluded from public life much longer. He will not want this benefaction to be attributed some day to the passage of time rather than to him.

So much for Caesar. Now let me tell you about the present situation. No one is so hostile to that cause which Pompey undertook (with better intentions than ability) as

45

to venture to call us disloyal citizens or unprincipled men. In this connection I am constantly struck by Caesar's sober, fair and wise behavior. He never, for example, speaks of Pompey except in the most honorable terms. "Yet," you will object, "he has taken many a harsh action against him as a public figure." But those were acts of war and victory, not of Caesar. See, in contrast, how he has embraced us. Cassius he made his legate, Brutus governor of Gaul, Sulpicius of Greece. Marcellus, with whom he was especially angry, he restored with full honors.

Where, then, is all this heading? In the nature of things the political situation will not tolerate — the system of government, whether it remains as is or changes, will not allow — first, that all men in the same condition not have equal treatment and fortune; and secondly, that good men and good citizens, unsullied by an ignominy, should not return to a state to which so many convicted of heinous crimes have already been allowed to return.

There is my augury for you. Had I the slightest doubt [of your return] . . . I would describe to you in what a general state of chaos and disorder we are living, since one perforce misses a state past recovery less than a well-ordered one. But there is no need for anything of that sort. We shall soon see you, as I hope, or rather as I clearly perceive, freed from restrictions. Meanwhile, to you in your absence and to your son who is here — that most constant and excellent replica of your body and soul — I have long since promised and devoted my zeal, service, attention, exertion, and I now do so the more as every day Caesar treats me in more friendly fashion and his friends lionize me like nobody else.[30] Any influence or favor I gain with him I will exert for you. And you, for your part, see that you keep up not only your courage but also the brightest hope.

Cicero, *Correspondence with Friends*, Book 4, no. 4

The addressee of this letter, at this time governor in Greece, had been consul in 51 B.C. together with Marcus Claudius Marcellus. The latter had been particularly active in attempting to thwart Caesar's rise to power. Nevertheless, in 46 B.C. Caesar consented to his being allowed to return from Greece, whither he had fled with Pompey.

[Rome, October 46 B.C.]
Cicero to Servius Sulpicius Rufus, greeting.
Everything here is in a complete mess, the dispirited ruins of a most abominable war. As a result everyone thinks that the place he is in is the most miserable, and that is why you regret your decision [to accept the appointment in Greece], thinking that we who are at home are the lucky ones, while to us you appear not completely free of annoyances, to be sure, but fortunate compared with ourselves. Your situation is better than ours in the very fact that you are free to write what's bothering you, while we cannot do even that safely — the fault for which lies not with the victor, who is the quintessence of moderation, but with the victory itself, which in civil wars is always outrageous.

The one respect in which I do have the advantage of you is in knowing a little ahead of you about the recall of your [consular] colleague Marcellus; in fact I even witnessed how the affair was managed . . . After complaining of Marcellus' "bitter hostility", as he called it, in contrast to your fairness and good sense which he praised in most flattering terms, Caesar said suddenly and unexpectedly that even despite a foreboding he would not refuse the senate's petition for Marcellus. The senate had arranged it thus, that Lucius Piso would bring up the case of Marcus Marcellus, Gaius Marcellus would immediately throw himself at Caesar's feet, and the senate to a man would then rise and approach Caesar as suppliants. Don't look too closely but that day looked so beautiful to me that I thought I saw some semblance of the republic reviving, as it were. A vote of thanks to Caesar was endorsed by one speaker after another — by all, in fact, except Volcacius, who said that he in Caesar's place would not have done it. As for me, I had previously resolved — not because I was indifferent but because I no longer had my former position of leadership — to hold my peace forever more. But I now changed my mind, and what shattered my determination was Caesar's magnanimity and the senate's deference. And so when my turn came I delivered, at some length, a speech of gratitude to Caesar; and by doing so I fear me I have surrendered for other public business as well that dignified

47

abstention which was my one consolation in a time of misfortunes. Still, now that I have avoided offending a man who, if I remained forever silent, might think I felt this was no republic, I can hereafter play a modest, restrained public role in such a way as to satisfy his wish and my interests. . . .

Cicero, *Speech on Behalf of Marcellus*, chapter 32

This, among Cicero's shortest extant speeches, probably took no more than fifteen minutes to deliver. What it lacks in length, however, it makes up for in fulsomeness. It begins by hailing Caesar for "such great kindness, such exceptional and unheard-of clemency, such great moderation while holding supreme power, such incredible and almost divine wisdom." Along the way Cicero expatiates on how he had always been for peace — one of his favorite themes in the post-Pharsalus period — and just before concluding he adds:

But now all dissension has been dispelled by arms and snuffed out by the victor's fairness. It remains now for all who have a bit of common sense — let alone wisdom — to be united in purpose. Only if you, Gaius Caesar, are safe and persevere in that policy which you have exhibited in the past and most especially today, only then can we be safe. Therefore all of us, since we want the present state of affairs to remain safe, urge and beseech you to look to your own life and safety. And, since you think there lurks some danger to be guarded against, I can speak for all the other senators as well as for myself in promising that we will provide you not only with watchmen and bodyguards, but with the bulwark of our own massed bodies.

Cicero, *Correspondence with Friends*, Book 6, no. 14

Quintus Ligarius had been the leader of the Pompeian forces in Africa. Encouraged by Caesar's pardon of Marcellus, Cicero undertook to obtain Ligarius' recall as well.

[Rome, 26 November 46 B.C.]
Cicero to Ligarius, greeting.
Be assured that I am devoting my every effort, all my pains and care and endeavor, to your welfare. For not only have I always had the greatest affection for you, but also the outstanding loyalty and love shown you by your brothers,

whom I embrace along with you in my kindest regard, allow me to let pass no occasion or opportunity for zealous service to you. What I am doing and have done for you I prefer that you learn from their letters rather than mine. But what I hope, trust and regard as settled regarding your recall, that I want to explain to you myself. . . .

At your brothers' request I accompanied them this morning to Caesar's levee and I put up with all the indignity and vexation of obtaining admission to speak with him. While your brothers and relatives lay prostrate at his feet, I stated the merits of your case and position. From Caesar's tone, which was definitely gentle and sympathetic, from the look in his eye and on his face, and from many signs besides which were easier for me to observe than to describe, I came away convinced in my own mind that there is no doubt about your recall.

Therefore keep up your spirits and courage, and, as you bore the stormiest weather philosophically, so now bear calmer times happily. And I will continue to attend to your interests as if they still required great effort, most willingly supplicating not only Caesar but also all his friends, who I know are most friendly to me. Farewell.

Cicero, *Speech on Behalf of Quintus Ligarius,* chapters 32-38

Before Caesar could act on the plea of Cicero and Ligarius' brothers, a personal enemy brought a charge of treason against Ligarius. Caesar took personal jurisdiction of the case, which was heard in the open forum. Cicero's speech in Ligarius' defense was rather brief — probably twenty minutes or so in delivery — but is reported to have had a great effect: according to Plutarch [*Life of Cicero* chapter 39], Caesar, who began the proceedings by referring to Ligarius as a "villain and an enemy," in the end "was moved [by Cicero's eloquence] to acquit the man of the charge." Ligarius repaid Caesar by becoming one of his assassins.

The peroration of Cicero's speech, one of his masterpieces of word-juggling, follows.

In saving Quintus Ligarius you will certainly gratify many of your own friends. . . . Need I speak of his brothers? Do not imagine, Caesar, that a single man's head is at stake here: either you must retain the three Ligarii in the community, or you must cast out the three. For in their view any exile is preferable to enjoying country and home and household gods while that one brother alone remains in exile. . . .

We heard you say repeatedly that while we [Pompeians] regarded all who were not with us as enemies, you regarded all who were not against you as being on your side. Let that policy, which won you the victory, still prevail. . . . Let this, like all your other pronouncements, be found to be the exact truth.

If you could see deep into the likemindedness of the brothers Ligarii, you would decide that all the brothers were on your side. . . . In their disposition they were all with you. One was swept away by the storm [of civil war], but even if he had acted of set purpose he would still be like all those you have, despite that, been willing to spare. Say he did go to war, he did disagree not only with you but with his brothers — still these[31] are your own people pleading with you [in his behalf]. . . .[32]

Just the other day you did something in the senate in the case of a man of most distinguished family and career. Do the same today, here in the forum, in the case of these brothers so fully supported by this whole throng. As you granted [Marcellus] to the senate, so give [Ligarius] to the people, whose wishes you have always held most dear. And just as that day [in the senate] was most glorious for you and most joyous for the Roman people, I beg you, Gaius Caesar, do not hesitate to earn as often as possible an accolade comparable to that glory. Nothing has as great an appeal to the people as benevolence, and none of your very many virtues is more admirable or gratifying than your compassion. In nothing do men more nearly approach the gods than in granting deliverance to fellow men. Your good fortune contains nothing greater than the power, your nature nothing nobler than the wish, to spare as many as possible. A longer speech is perhaps called for by this case, but a shorter surely by your nature. With the thought, therefore, that it is far better for you to speak than for me or anyone else to hold the floor, I will now close. I add only this reminder, that if you grant the absent defendant his life, you will also be granting it to all these here present.

Cicero, *Letters to Atticus,* Book 13, no. 52

By the middle of 45 B.C. Cicero's disillusionment with Caesar was complete. On 17 May he had written to Atticus, "I'd rather see him *templé avec* Romulus" — who, according to legend, had died a violent death — "than with Safety." And toward the end of August, on hearing that Caesar was returning in triumph from Spain, he had written to another friend, "Our master is back sooner than we thought." In mid-December, while on an inspection tour of Campania, Caesar paused to dine with Cicero at the latter's villa near Puteoli. Here is Cicero's account.

[Puteoli, 19 December 45 B.C.]
Such a formidable guest! *mais pas de regrets.* In fact, it was all very pleasant. When he arrived at Philippus' yesterday evening, that villa was filled so chockful of soldiers that there was hardly a place free for Caesar himself to take his supper. Two thousand men, if you please! I was in a dither at what might happen [when he came to me] today, but Cassius Barba came to the rescue by giving me sentries. So the soldiers had to make camp in the open, and my villa was protected.

Today Caesar remained at Philippus' till about one o'clock, admitting no one (going over accounts with Balbus, I imagine). Then he took a walk along the shore [and came to my villa]. After two he went to his bath . . . was anointed, and took his place at dinner. He was following a regimen of emetics, and so he both ate and drank *sans peur* and with relish. It was really a very good dinner, well served, and not only that but

"well cooked and seasoned, with good table talk — in fact, a pleasure."

In addition, *son entourage* was accommodated right lavishly in three dining rooms. Even the lowlier freedmen and slaves wanted for nothing, and the grander ones I entertained in style. In a word, I showed I was a man of parts. Even so, he is hardly the kind of guest to whom one would say, "My dear fellow, do stop in again on your way back." Once is enough. Our talk? *rien de sérieux,*[34] lots of *entretien érudit.* In short, he was pleased and enjoyed himself. He said he would spend a day at Puteoli, another at Baiae.

There you have it — call it hospitality or *logement*. I found it a bit inconvenient, as I have said, but not seriously trying.

Suetonius, *Life of the Deified Julius Caesar*, chapter 75

He showed admirable moderation and clemency both in his conduct of the civil war and after his victory. Whereas Pompey thundered that he would regard anyone who failed to join the government side as an enemy, Caesar proclaimed that he would count neutrals who joined neither party among his friends. He even offered all those whom he had named to the post of centurion on Pompey's recommendation an opportunity to go over to him. At Ilerda, when terms of surrender were being discussed and the two armies were in continuous contact and communication, [the Pompeian lieutenants] Afranius and Petreius in a sudden about-face killed the Caesarian soldiers who happened to be in their camp. But Caesar refused to imitate such treachery. On the contrary, at the battle of Pharsalus he urged his men to spare their fellow-citizens, and after the battle he allowed every one of his men to choose, if he wished, one of the other side to save. And you will find that, with the exception of Afranius, Faustus and Lucius Caesar junior, no Pompeian lost his life except in battle, and even those three are not believed to have been put to death by his order, even though the first two had taken up arms again after being pardoned, and the third had cruelly killed off freedmen and slaves of Caesar's with fire and sword, and had even butchered the animals Caesar had purchased for a public spectacle. Finally, toward the end of his life he even allowed all whom he had not yet pardoned to return to Italy, even to hold magistracies and military commands. He even reerected the statues of Lucius Sulla and Pompey that the populace had smashed. Thereafter he preferred to disarm rather than punish any dangerous plots or expressions of opposition. Thus, when conspiracies or nocturnal gatherings were detected, he took no action beyond issuing an edict to say he knew of them; and when people criticized him sharply he contented himself with warning them in a public assembly to stop it. So

too he bore with urbanity the savage attacks on his reputation in Aulus Caecina's most slanderous pamphlet and
Pitholaus' most abusive verses.[35]

Plutarch, *Life of Julius Caesar*, chapter 57

So the Romans bowed before his good fortune, accepted
the bit and, deeming his sole rule a respite from the civil
wars and attendant miseries, they appointed him dictator
for life. This was admittedly a tyranny, as the monarchy
now added permanence to absolutism. The first honors,
proposed in the senate by Cicero, were quite well within
mortal bounds. But other men went to excess, trying to
outdo one another, and the result was that Caesar became
odious and offensive to even the mildest of men because
of the extraordinary pretension of the honors voted him.
It is generally thought that those who hated Caesar no less
than his flatterers cooperated in this, in order to have as
many grievances as possible against him and present the
most serious accusations to justify an attack on his life.

Now in all other respects, after ending the civil wars,
he showed himself above reproach, and certainly it does
not seem inappropriate for them to have voted a temple
to Clemency in thanks for his moderation. For he pardoned
many of those who had fought against him in the wars,
and to some he even gave offices and honors in addition
— for example to Brutus and Cassius, both of whom were
now praetors. And he did not overlook the statues of Pompey that had been thrown down, but had them set up
again — at which Cicero remarked that Caesar by erecting
Pompey's statues had firmly planted his own. When his
friends urged him to have a bodyguard and many of them
volunteered for it, he would not allow them, saying it was
better to meet death once and for all than to be always
expecting it.

Suetonius, *Life of the Deified Julius Caesar*, chapters 37-44

After defeating Scipio [in Africa] and ending the wars he
celebrated five triumphs, four a few days apart in a single
month, and another by itself after he overcame Pompey's
sons [in Spain]. The first and most outstanding triumph

was the Gallic, second the Alexandrian, then the Pontic, after that the African, and last the Spanish, each with its distinctive panoply and ornament. On the day of the Gallic triumph an axle broke as he rode through the Velabrum and he was nearly thrown from the chariot, so he walked up to the Capitol by torchlight, flanked by forty elephants bearing lamps. Among the displays of the Pontic triumph there was carried a three-word inscription, VENI•VIDI•VICI ["I came, I saw, I conquered"] — not, as in the others, celebrating the feats of the war, but emphasizing the speed of its completion.

To each and every foot-soldier in his veteran legions he gave, over and above the 2,000 sesterces he had paid them at the beginning of the civil disturbance, another 24,000 sesterces by way of booty. He also assigned them lands, but not contiguous plots, so as not to dispossess completely any of the existing owners. To the civilian population he distributed ten modii of grain and a like number of pounds of oil per man, as well as the 300 sesterces that he had once promised, plus another 100 to compensate for the delay. He also remitted a year's house rent up to 2,000 sesterces in Rome, up to 500 in Italy. He added a banquet and a distribution of meat, and after the Spanish victory two dinners: the first having been rather stinted, to his way of thinking, and not in keeping with his usual liberality, he laid on another five days later on a most lavish scale.

He entertained them with every kind of show: a gladiatorial combat; actors performing in all languages all over the city, in every precinct; also races in the circus, athletic contests, naval war games. At the combat in the forum Furius Leptinus, who came from a praetorian family, and Quintus Calpenus, a senator and quondam barrister, fought to the finish.[36] A Pyrrhic dance was performed by sons of the princes of Asia and Bithynia. At the plays Decimus Laberius, a Roman eques, after performing a farce of his own composition, was rewarded with a gift of 500,000 sesterces and the gold ring . . . At the races, after the circus was lengthened at both ends and a circular canal dug, young men of the noblest houses drove in four-horse and two-horse chariots, and raced on horseback, vaulting from horse to horse as they rode. The game of Troy was performed by two companies of younger and older boys. Wild-animal combats were staged for five days, and the grand finale was a battle between two opposing battle-divisions, with 500 foot-soldiers, 20 elephants and 30 cavalry on each side. To make more room for this fight the goalposts were removed from the circus, and in their places the two opposing camps were pitched. The athletic contests, held in a temporary stadium built for the occasion over by the Campus Martius, lasted three days. The naval battle, held in an artificial lake dug in the lesser Codeta, presented a clash of bi-, tri- and quadriremes of the Tyrian and Egyptian fleets carrying a large number of fighting men. Such huge throngs of people streamed in from all over to all of these spectacles, that many visitors had to sleep in tents pitched in streets and alleyways, and often there was such crowding that many, including two senators, were crushed to death.

Caesar then turned to governmental reorganization. First he reformed the calendar, which, through the fault of the pontiffs in their wilful intercalations, had long been so dislocated that the harvest festival no longer came in summer nor the vintage festival in the autumn.[37] He tied the year to the course of the sun, giving it 365 days plus [instead of an intercalary month] one day to be intercalated every fourth year. And to make the future time reckoning correct from the next January 1st, he added two months between November and December, which, with the month already intercalated in this according to the old practice, made this a year of fifteen months.

He filled vacancies in the senate, created additional patricians, increased the number of praetors, aediles, quaestors and even lesser magistrates, reinstated men who had been stripped of privilege by action of censors or who had been condemned for electoral bribery by jury verdict. He shared the elections with the people so that, leaving out the candidates for the consulship, from the remaining number of candidates half the appointees would be the people's choice, the other half his own nominees. To make his nominations he sent the tribes missives with brief messages: "Caesar the dictator to such-and-such tribe. I com-

55

mend to you AB and CD, to hold their offices by your vote." He admitted to office even the sons of the proscribed. He limited jury service to two classes, the equestrian and senatorial, eliminating a third, the tribunes of the treasury.

He took a census of the populace, but not in the traditional way or place. Instead he enrolled them street by street, assisted in this by the tenement owners, and he thus reduced the number receiving public grain from 320,000 to 150,000. And to eliminate the possibility of their holding meetings in the future for additional enrolments, he provided that each year a praetor should draw lots from among the unenrolled to fill the places of the recipients who had died.

With 80,000 citizens transferred to overseas colonies, he sought to maintain the depleted population of the city by providing that no citizen older than twenty or younger than forty might absent himself from Italy for more than three years in a row unless detained on military service; that no senator's son should go abroad except as a companion or staff officer of a magistrate; that men engaged in cattle raising should see that not fewer than one-third of their shepherds were freeborn men. He conferred citizenship upon all who practised medicine at Rome and upon all teachers of the liberal arts, that they might the more willingly live in the city and others like them be eager to come.

As for debts, he dashed any hope of their outright cancellation — a repeated popular demand[38] — but did go so far as to decree that debtors could satisfy creditors at the value at which they had acquired the goods before the civil war,[39] and could deduct from that principal of the loan any interest paid in cash or by bank transfer. These provisions reduced outstanding debt by about one-fourth.

He dissolved all associations except those founded in remote antiquity.[40] He increased the penalties for crimes, notably against the rich: they had involved themselves in capital offenses with relative freedom because they could [if convicted] simply go into exile with their fortunes intact, but now he punished murderers, as Cicero writes, with confiscation of their entire estate, and the others with confiscation of half.

He administered justice with the most rigorous care. Men convicted of extortion he removed from the senatorial order. He annulled the nuptials of an ex-praetor because, even though there was no suspicion of adultery, he had married the woman the very day after her divorce. He introduced tariffs on imported wares. He banned the use of litters and the wearing of scarlet robes and pearls except by persons of certain standings or ages on specified days. He took exceptional measures to enforce the sumptuary law, stationing inspectors about the market with instructions to seize and bring to him delicacies that violated the ordinance, and sometimes, when some such wares had gotten by his inspectors, sending lictors or soldiers to remove them from the dining rooms where they were being served.

For the embellishment and modernization of the city, as well as for the protection and extension of the empire, he devised more and greater designs every day. The principal ones were: to build a temple to Mars, the biggest anywhere, after filling in and levelling off the lake where the naval combat had been staged, and to build also a theater of very great size up against the Tarpeian Rock; to reduce the civil law to a fixed code, collecting in a very few volumes the best and essential out of the enormous, diffuse accumulation of laws; to create public libraries with the greatest possible number of Greek and Latin books, with Marcus Varro put in charge of buying and arranging them; to drain the Pomptine marshes; to make an outlet for Lake Fucinus; to build a highway from the Adriatic over the ridge of the Apennines all the way to the Tiber; to cut a canal through the Isthmus [of Corinth]; to check the Dacians, who had poured into Pontus and Thrace; after that to invade Parthia by way of Armenia and try a few skirmishes before risking an all-out attack.

Such were the projects he was engaged in or planning when death intervened.

The Conspiracy and Assassination

Appian, *The Civil Wars*, Book 4, section 134
This was no ordinary crime, nor one of small scope. It was committed unexpectedly against a friend; ungratefully against a benefactor who had shown mercy after a war; lawlessly against a sovereign; in a senate chamber; against a pontiff wearing his priestly garb; against a ruler who was unique and useful beyond all men to his country and its empire.

Following, in the chronological order of their authors, are the six principal accounts of the conspiracy and assassination that have survived from ancient times. There is an obvious fascination in reading them in sequence, comparing the political attitudes of the writers, noting their emphases and omissions, observing the details common to or unique in the several accounts. For the modern reader looking for the "truth" of the matter there is also frustration. To take one example: Marcus Brutus has generally been regarded, through the ages, as having been the leading spirit of the coup; but Plutarch says it was Cassius, and Nicolaus of Damascus, the only one of these writers who was alive at the time, implies it was Decimus Brutus. Which of these appraisals is, or more closely reflects, the truth of the matter? We will never know. So too with the argument over kingship, or tyranny — by which the Romans of that time meant the arbitrary or arrogant exercise of great power or office (cf. above, p. 53) — or over the diadem that turned up one day adorning Caesar's statue on the rostra. As a distinguished historian recently put it, "The truth about the *diadema* will forever remain uncertain. Did Caesar's enemies stand behind the decoration campaign in order to damage Caesar's reputation? Did Caesar secretly authorize the deed in order to test the public mood? The problem is even more involved. . . ."[41]

The reader of the following pages will no doubt be struck by the fact that at some points two or more of the accounts show practically verbatim identity, clear-cut evidence that those passages derive from a common source. It may be helpful to recall that of the five authors Nicolaus was about twenty years old (but had not yet come to Rome) on 15 March 44 B.C., while the others lived and wrote some fifty to 250 years after the event.

Nicolaus of Damascus, *Life of Augustus,* chapters 14, 20, 23

The conspiracy, at first confined to but a few, soon became more extensive than any other that history records against a ruler. The number of those who were in on it is said to have been more than eighty. Among the principals were Decimus Brutus, a close friend of Caesar's; Gaius Cassius; and the same Marcus Brutus who passed at Rome for one of the most virtuous of men. All of them had been supporters of Pompey, and had fought against Caesar. Fallen, after the defeat of their leader, into the hands of his rival, they were allowed to live their lives in complete security. For no one knew better than Caesar how to win hearts with kindness, making fear give way to hope. His character was full of mildness, and he bore no grudge against the vanquished. But they, abusing Caesar's quiet trust, used it against him, surrounding him — the better to hide their plots — with seductive flattery and hypocritical adulation.

Of the motives impelling the conspirators some were personal, others general. Some of the conspirators hoped to take Caesar's place after removing him. Others still smarted from their defeat in the civil war, from loss of patrimony or riches, or even from the level of the offices they held at Rome. But, concealing their anger under more specious pretexts, they protested that they could not endure to be ruled by one man but wanted to be governed by laws equal for all.

In sum, first the most powerful were driven by variously engendered grievances to form the plot. Then, others were drawn to it by personal resentment or party spirit, which assured their friends of their absolutely dependable support. Finally, there were some who, without any such motives, were simply attracted by the authority of those illustrious figures and placed themselves at their side. These,

59

though outraged at seeing the republican government supplanted by the power of one man, would not themselves have started a revolution; but once others had made the first move they were all ready to back these bold men and even, if necessary, to share their dangers.

Another powerful factor was the ancient family of the Bruti, so proud of the glory of their ancestors who founded the republic after overthrowing the monarchy that had been established by Romulus. Also, Caesar's old friends were becoming disaffected at seeing their former enemies, whose lives he had spared, now being honored equally with themselves. Even those he had thus rehabilitated were far from well disposed: their inveterate hatred stifled any feeling of gratitude in them and they ceaselessly recalled, not that Caesar had spared their lives and heaped benefactions upon them, but all the goods they had lost after their defeat; and this intensified their rage. In fact many a one, though Caesar was at pains never to wound anyone's self-respect, was filled with rancor by the very fact that he owed him his life. They were constantly plagued by the thought, ever present in their minds, that they owed to his benefaction what they could easily have obtained on their own had they but been victorious.

Furthermore, even the various classes of soldiery were far from content. The majority had simply returned to private life after so many hard campaigns. But the officers felt cheated of the honors due them, since the defeated had been incorporated into the ranks of the veterans and were receiving the same rewards. Caesar's friends could not bear being placed on a par with their former prisoners, some of whom, they saw, were even obtaining rewards at their expense. . . . Finally, Caesar himself, rightly proud of his many brilliant victories and behaving as if he were superhuman, was a cynosure to the people but an object of hate and envy to the grandees, the men who aspired to power.

Thus there were leagued against him men of every condition, great and small, friends and enemies, soldiers and civilians. Each one advanced his own particular pretexts for entering into the conspiracy, and used his personal grievances to lend credence to the complaints of others.

They vied in inciting one another, finding reciprocal confidence in the fact that each had his own private grievance against Caesar. That is why no one, in a conspiracy numbering so many, ventured to commit a single betrayal. Though it has been said that a few minutes before his death Caesar was handed a paper containing an account of the conspiracy, but he was not able to read it and he was still holding it in his hand when he was assassinated. It was found among his papers. . . .

Since Caesar had never been defeated in the 302 battles he had fought in Europe and Asia, he was generally regarded as invincible. But the conspirators felt confident of success, for, seeing that he often went out alone, they expected they could kill him in an ambush. They therefore sought every means of separating him from his bodyguard. They flattered him, told him he ought to be universally regarded as sacrosanct and be called father of his country. They even had laws passed to such effect, hoping that he would be led by their protestations of devotion to consider his popularity a sufficient shield and dismiss his bodyguard. Once they had accomplished this they would find a thousand opportunities to carry out their undertaking with ease. . . .

The meetings at which they laid their plans were never held openly of course. They would go secretly, a few at a time, to one or another's house, and at those gatherings they discussed many different proposals, including the place and means to effect their purpose. Some were for falling upon him on the Sacred Way, where he passed often. Other thought it better to wait for the elections . . . to get to which Caesar would have to cross a bridge; here the conspirators would divide the work — while some pushed him over the side, others would be waiting below to finish him off. Still other proposed executing their plan at the approaching gladiatorial games, when they could appear armed in public without arousing the least suspicion. But the majority agreed to attack him in the senate, where he would be alone and they in great numbers; and as for weapons, they could hide daggers under their togas. . . .

When the agreed-upon day arrived, the conspirators

gathered, all prepared, in the portico of Pompey, whither they had already been summoned more than once. Then, showing how everything on earth is uncertain and subject to her caprice, Fate led Caesar to that portico, where presently he would lie lifeless before the statue of the very Pompey over whom he had triumphed when alive. But now the victor in his turn would fall, struck down before the bust of that rival now dead. Surely one must see the hand of all-powerful Fate in all these events.

Plutarch, *Life of Brutus*, chapters 10-17 [selections]
When Cassius sounded his friends regarding an attempt on Caesar, they all agreed provided Brutus headed it. Such an enterprise, they felt, would lack neither hands nor resolve, but the reputation of a man like him would sanctify, as it were, and by his very presence guarantee the justice of the act. Otherwise, they would act with less zeal and after the act would be the more suspect, for Brutus, people would say, would not have dissociated himself from the deed if it had had a just cause. After mulling this over, Cassius visited Brutus . . . and asked him whether he intended to be at the meeting of the senate on the first of March, when, he had learned, Caesar's friends would introduce a motion that he be made king. Brutus said he would not attend the meeting. "But what," asked Cassius, "if he summons us?" "Then it will be my business," said Brutus, "not to remain silent but to defend my country and die before liberty does." In great elation Cassius said, "But what Roman will suffer you so to die? Brutus, do you not know yourself? Do you think the graffiti on your tribunal are the work of weavers and shopkeepers, and not of our leading and most influential men? From other praetors people expect handouts, spectacles, gladiators, but from you they expect what you owe your ancestry — the overthrow of tyranny. And they are ready to undergo every trial for you, if you but show yourself the kind of man they think and expect." He then embraced and kissed Brutus, and thus reconciled they turned to rounding up their friends.

A certain Gaius Ligarius was among the friends of Pompey, and though denounced as such he had been pardoned by Caesar. This man, feeling no gratitude for his release from prosecution but aggrieved at the power that had placed him in jeopardy, was an enemy of Caesar and one of Brutus' most intimate friends. Visiting when he was sick, Brutus said, "O Ligarius, what a time this is for you to be sick!" And he, at once raising himself on his elbow, took Brutus by his right hand and said, "O Brutus, if your intentions are worthy of yourself, I feel just fine."

After that they secretly sounded out those of the nobles whom they trusted, filled them in and recruited them. They chose not only their intimates but all whom they knew to be intrepid, courageous and contemptuous of death. That is why they concealed what they were doing from Cicero: even though he was paramount among them in the confidence and good will he enjoyed, they were afraid that, as he was by nature indisposed to daring, had with the passage of time acquired the circumspection of old age, and was given to calculating every detail in everything with a view to maximum safety, he might blunt the cutting edge of their purpose when swift action was called for. Brutus also left out other friends, notably Statilius the Epicurean and [the Stoic] Favonius, a devoted follower of Cato, because some time before, when he had indirectly tested them on some such question in a philosophical discussion, Favonius had answered that a civil war was worse than an unlawful monarchy and Statilius had said it was pointless for a philosopher or man of intelligence to take any risk or trouble on account of ordinary, unintelligent people. . . . It was decided to bring in the other Brutus, surnamed Albinus, who was not particularly dynamic or courageous but was valuable because he was maintaining a gang of gladiators for a Roman spectacle, and he was a trusted friend of Caesar's. When Cassius and Labeo[42] talked to him he gave them no answer but sought out Brutus in private and, on learning that he was the leader of the affair, readily agreed to cooperate. It was Brutus' reputation that brought in the majority and the best of the others as well. And even though they did not bind themselves by mutual oaths or sacred pledges, they all kept it to themselves and were so successful in maintaining silence and working together to the end that, although the deed was forecast by the gods in prophecies, portents and sacrifices, no one lent any credence. . . .

When a meeting of the senate was scheduled to which Caesar was expected to come, they decided to make their move: then, they reasoned, they could be together en masse without arousing suspicion, and they would have close at hand all the best and leading men, who, once the great deed was done, would straightway join the side of liberty. And it seemed to them that the meeting place was also providentially in their favor, since it was one of the porticoes near the theater, containing a hall in which stood a statue of Pompey, erected by the city in his honor for adorning that area with his porticoes and theater. To this place, then, the senate was summoned for right about the middle of the month of March — the Romans call that day the Ides of March — as if some divine power were leading the man to Pompey's vengeance.

When the day came Brutus tucked a dagger under his cloak (only his wife knew it) and went out. The others assembled at Cassius' house and conducted his son, who was assuming the so-called "man's toga," into the forum. From there they all hastened to the portico of Pompey and waited, expecting Caesar to come to the senate any minute. Then indeed anyone who knew what was afoot would have been amazed at the impassivity of the men on the very brink of their dread act. Some, being praetors, had to give audience, and they not only listened calmly, patiently, as if they had all the time in the world, to the petitioners and disputants, but even took great pains to give their decision in every case precisely and appropriately. One man, refusing to accept a verdict [by Brutus], appealed to Caesar with many a loud cry and protestation; whereupon Brutus turned to the bystanders and said, "Caesar does not prevent and will not prevent me from acting in accordance with the laws."

And yet there was much to upset them in the course of events, first and foremost the fact that, though the day was advancing, Caesar was tarrying at home, detained by his wife and prevented by the soothsayers from going out because the omens were unfavorable. Then too, someone came up to Casca, one of the conspirators, and shaking his hand said, "You hid the secret from us, Casca, but Brutus has told me everything." And as Casca looked panic-stricken the man added with a laugh, "Where, my friend, did you suddenly get so rich as to become a candidate for the aedileship?" Thus Casca, nonplussed by the ambiguity [of the initial remark], came within a hair of blurting out the secret. Again, a senator, Popilius Laenas, greeted Brutus and Cassius more warmly than usual and whispered quietly, "I join you in praying that you may accomplish what you have in mind, and I urge you not to delay, for the matter is no secret." Saying which he departed, and his words filled them with suspicion that their enterprise had been found out. At this juncture, too, someone came running from Brutus' house to tell him his wife was dead. . . . Brutus was naturally overcome at the report just brought him, but he by no means abandoned the common cause or retreated, in his suffering, into his private grief.

And now came word that Caesar was approaching, borne on a litter. Dispirited at the omens, he had decided not to sanction any major business that day but to postpone any such, pleading indisposition. As he stepped from the litter Popilius Laenas — the same who a little earlier had wished Brutus and his associates a successful outcome — rushed up and engaged him in conversation for a considerable time, and Caesar stood and listened attentively. The confederates — to dub them thus — could not catch what Laenas what saying, but convinced by their own suspicions that the conversation was a betrayal of their plot, they scrapped their plans, looked at one another and by their expressions mutually agreed that they must not wait around to be arrested but should at once take their own lives. Cassius and some others had already clasped their daggers beneath their togas and were already drawing them, when Brutus realized from Laenas' bearing that he was earnestly asking, not informing. Brutus did not say anything, because there were so many non-conspirators about, but with a beaming expression he spread encouragement to the Cassius group. And after a little Laenas kissed Caesar's hand and withdrew, thus making it clear that he had accosted Caesar on behalf of himself and a matter concerning himself.

The senate preceded Caesar into the hall, and the conspirators took up positions around Caesar's chair as if intending to petition him in some matter. Cassius is said to have turned his face toward Pompey's statue and called on it, as if it were sentient, to help. Trebonius drew Antony aside at the door and detained him outside in conversation. As Caesar entered the senate rose in his honor, but as soon as he was seated the conspirators surrounded him in a tight pack. Tillius Cimber was thrust forward to please for his brother in exile, and they all joined in his plea, clutching Caesar's hands, kissing his breast and head. At first he kept rejecting their pleas, but then, as they would not desist, he tried to shake them off and stand up; whereupon Tillius with both hands tore Caesar's toga from his shoulders and Casca, who was standing behind Caesar, drew his dagger and struck the first blow — near the shoulder, and not deep. Caesar caught the dagger by the handle and shouted, in Latin, "Vile Casca, what do you think you're doing?" Casca, speaking in Greek, called on his brother to help. Caesar, riddled by now with many wounds, was looking around for a way to escape, but when he saw Brutus coming at him with dagger drawn, he let go of Casca's hand that he was still holding fast, covered his head with his toga and surrendered his body to the blows. The conspirators thrashed about the body without letup, and striking with their many daggers they kept wounding one another (Brutus, for example, received a cut on the hand as he tried to join in the murder), and all were covered with blood.

Plutarch, *Life of Caesar*, chapters 62-66

. . . Caesar was actually suspicious of Cassius, and he once said to his friends, "What do you think Cassius wants? I'm not too happy with him, he looks too pale." And again, when Antony and Dolabella were denounced to him as planning a coup, he is quoted as saying, "I am not much afraid of these fat, long-haired fellows, but rather of those pale, thin types," meaning Cassius and Brutus.

But that which is fated is not, it seems, so much unexpected as unavoidable. Amazing signs and portents are said to have appeared. There were lights in the sky, loud noises reverberating everywhere at night, solitary birds descending upon the forum. Perhaps these are not worth mentioning in relation to such a memorable event, but Strabo the philosopher reports that many men, glowing as if on fire, appeared to be attacking; that the slave of a military man tossed a huge ball of fire from his hand and appeared to the onlookers to be burning, but when the fire died down he appeared uninjured; that when Caesar himself was sacrificing the victim's heart was found to be missing — a terrifying omen, since in the nature of things no animal could survive without a heart. Many also relate the following: that a soothsayer forewarned him to guard against a great danger on the day in the month of March that the Romans call the Ides; and when the day had come Caesar, on his way to senate, greeted the soothsayer and said to him in jest, "Well, the Ides of March are at hand," and the other calmly replied, "Yes, they are at hand, but they are not past."

On the day before, while dining at Marcus Lepidus', he happened as usual to be signing some letters while reclining at table when the conversation turned to the different ways of dying and asked what kind of death was the best, to which he blurted out before the rest could speak, "An unexpected one." That night, as he was sleeping as usual beside his wife, the doors and windows of the bedroom flew open all together, and Caesar, although dazed by their banging and by the light of the moon shining down on him, noticed that Calpurnia was fast asleep but uttering indistinct sounds and inarticulate groans in her dreams: she dreamt, in fact, that she was weeping over him as she held him, slaughtered, in her arms. (There are those who say this was not what she dreamt. Their version is that there was a gable ornament which, according to Livy, had been placed on Caesar's house by decree of the senate as a symbol of reverence, and Calpurnia dreamt she saw that being torn down, which is why she was groaning and weeping.)

When day came, she begged Caesar to put off the senate and not to stir out if at all possible, and if he made light of her dreams to consult sacrifices and other divination about what lay ahead. It appears that he too was prey to some suspicion and fear, because he had never before perceived any womanish inclination toward superstition in Calpurnia, whom he now saw in great distress. And so, when the seers reported to him that the signs were inauspicious even after many sacrifices, he decided to send Antony to dissolve the senate.

But at that point Decimus Brutus surnamed Albinus, who was so trusted by Caesar as to have been entered in his will as alternate heir but nevertheless participated in the conspiracy together with the other Brutus and Cassius, fearing that if Caesar escaped them that day their business would be discovered, scoffed at the seers and chided Caesar with courting blame and disparagement from the senators. They would think he was holding them in derision, because they had come at his bidding and were all set to vote unanimously that he be named king of all the provinces outside Italy, entitled to wear a diadem everywhere, on land or sea, when traveling abroad. But if someone should bring them word to dissolve their sitting for now and meet again when Calpurnia was lucky enough to have better dreams, you can imagine the kinds of things his detractors would say, and who would listen to his friends arguing that this wasn't slavery and tyranny? So, even if he was absolutely convinced, said Brutus, that it was a day for expiation [which precluded the transaction of public business], 'twere better that he go in person to greet the senate before adjourning it. As he spoke Brutus took Caesar by the hand and led him out. When he had gone but a little way from his door, a slave — not one of his — tried to get to him but was frustrated by the jostling crowd around Caesar; whereupon he forced his way into the house and turned himself over to Calpurnia, begging her to keep him safe till Caesar's return as he had important information to give him.

Artemidorus, a Cnidian by birth, and a teacher of Greek philosophy — which is how he had gotten to be on intimate terms with some of Brutus' coterie, and thus to know a good bit of what they were up to — came to Caesar bringing a small papyrus roll containing what he wanted to disclose. He had observed that each time Caesar received such a paper he handed to his attendants. He therefore managed to get right up close and said, "Read this one, Caesar, by yourself, and at once. It is a message about matters of moment that concern you directly." Caesar took it, and tried a number of times to read it, but was prevented by the sheer numbers of the petitioners about him, and he was still holding it in his hand — the only one he retained — when he passed on into the senate chamber. Some say it was another who handed him that roll, because Artemidorus simply could not get to him but was shoved away all along the route.

All this might have happened by mere chance. But the place where that murder was enacted — namely, the place where the senate was then assembled, which contained a statue of Pompey because Pompey had dedicated it as a decorative appurtenance to his theater — revealed to all and sundry that the deed occurred there at the guidance and bidding of some divine power. Indeed, it is also said that Cassius, just before the onset, looked toward Pompey's statue and silently invoked its aid; and Cassius was normally an adherent of the Epicurean philosophy, but it would appear that at this crisis, now that the terrible moment was at hand, his former cool logic gave way to emotional agitation.

Mark Antony, who was loyal to Caesar and physically strong, was detained outside the senate house by Brutus Albinus,[43] who purposely started a conversation that dragged on at great length. When Caesar went in the senate rose respectfully, and some of Brutus' confederates gathered round behind his chair while others went to meet him as if to join Tillius Cimber in petitioning for his exiled brother, and they added their pleas to his as they accompanied Caesar to his chair. After taking his seat he continued to reject their pleas, and as their importunities grew more impassioned he began to express his annoyance with them. Then Tillius Cimber grabbed his toga with both hands and pulled it down from his neck — which was the preconcerted signal for the attack. Casca was the first, striking Caesar with his dagger on the side of the neck — not a mortal blow or even a deep cut, no doubt because he was agitated, as was natural at the start of a great, bold venture. Caesar turned around, grabbed the dagger and kept hold of it. Then, practically at the same instant they both cried out, the one that was struck saying in Latin, "Damn you,

69

Casca, what do you think you're doing?" and the one that struck calling in Greek to this brother, "Brother, help!"

As the beginning thus unfolded, those not privy to the plot were filled with consternation and horror at what was going on, but they dared not flee, nor go to Caesar's aid, nor even so much as say a word. But those who had come prepared for the murder each held out his naked dagger, and Caesar, encircled and driven — whichever way he looked — by blows from all their weapons aimed at his face and eyes, was like a hunted animal entoiled in the hands of them all (for all had bound themselves to strike an actual blow and thus taste of the slaughter). Thus even Brutus gave him one blow, in the groin. Some writers say that Caesar fought desperately against the others, twisting his body this way and that and screaming, but when he saw that Brutus had drawn a dagger he pulled his toga down over his head and sank, either by chance or pushed by his killers, against the pedestal on which Pompey's statue stood. The murder liberally sprinkled the pedestal with blood, so that Pompey himself seemed to be presiding over the vengeance taken on his enemy, who now lay prostrate at his feet, quivering from a multitude of wounds. Twenty-three, to be exact, is the number he is supposed to have received, and many of the conspirators were wounded by one another as they rained so many blows upon a single body.

Suetonius, *Life of the Deified Julius Caesar*, chapters 79-87 [selections]

Various rumors had spread, one to the effect that he was going to leave the administration of the city to friends and move to Alexandria or Ilium, taking the empire's wealth with him and draining Italy's population by conscriptions; another, that at the next meeting of the senate Lucius Cotta, speaking for The Fifteen, would announce that it was recorded in the books of fate that the Parthians could not be conquered except by a king, and would introduce a motion, accordingly, that Caesar be given that title. This last was the reason why the conspirators accelerated the business in hand, so as to avoid having to give their consent.

And so the plots that had hitherto remained separate, often in groups of two or three men, all came together. The populace, too, was now unhappy at the state of affairs, and openly as well as privately criticized Caesar's rule and called for protectors. For example, when he enrolled foreigners in the senate a placard was posted, reading: "Great! Just nobody show a new senator the way to the senate house." And the following ditty was chanted everywhere:

"In triumph and then right into the senate Caesar leads the Gauls.
Off go their Gallic britches, on goes the senatorial tunic."

When Quintus Maximus, whom he had appointed consul suffect for three months, was entering the theater and his lictor sang out the customary call for respectful attention, he was greeted by jeer that was taken up by all, "Call him a consul?". . . . On the statue of Lucius Brutus someone wrote, "Would you were living," and on Caesar's:

"Brutus because he drove out the kings was our first consul,
This man because he drove out the consuls is our king back again."

More than sixty joined in the conspiracy against him, but the chiefs of the conspiracy were Gaius Cassius and Marcus and Decimus Brutus. . . . [Caesar entered the senate house and] as he took his seat the conspirators gathered round him as if to pay their respects. Then Tillius Cimber, also playing a principal role, approached as if to present a petition, and as Caesar with a shake of the head and a motion of the hand made to put him off to another time, he pulled Caesar's toga from both his shoulders. "Now you're going too far," cried Caesar, and at the same moment one of the Cascas stabbed him just below the collarbone. Caesar caught Casca's arm and jabbed it with his stylus, but as he tried to spring to his feet he was stopped by another blow. Seeing that he was beset on every side by daggers drawn, he wrapped his head in his toga and with his left hand pulled the lap of his toga down to his feet, so as to fall more decently, with the lower part of his body also covered. And thus shrouded he was riddled with three and twenty wounds, uttering nothing but a wordless groan at the first blow. There is of course the other tradition, repeated by some writers, that as Marcus Brutus fell upon him he said in Greek, "You too, my child?"

All fled, and he lay there lifeless for a time until three young slaves put him on a litter and carried him home, one arm hanging down. And among so many wounds none proved to be mortal, according to the physician Antistius, except the second he received in the chest. . . .

On one detail there is total agreement, that he met just about the kind of end he would have wanted. Once, after reading in Xenophon how Cyrus in his last illness had given instructions about his funeral, Caesar deprecated such a slow kind of death and expressed the wish that his would be sudden and swift. In fact, the day before he was killed, in a conversation that rose at dinner in Marcus Lepidus' house as to what was the most convenient way to die, he had plumped for a sudden and unexpected end.

Appian, *The Civil Wars*, Book 4, sections 111-117

Four days before his intended departure from Rome [to wage war in Parthia] his enemies slew him in the senate house. They acted either out of envy of his good fortune and power, now become altogether enormous, or, as they themselves alleged, out of a desire to restore the ancestral constitution and a fear — knowing him as they did — that if he added Parthia to his conquests he would undoubtedly become king. My own considered view is that they found in that title a convenient pretext for their conspiracy: the difference to them was one of name only, since in reality a dictator is exactly the same as a king.

Two men in particular organized the conspiracy. One was Marcus Brutus surnamed Caepio, son of the Brutus who lost his life in Sulla's time; after the disaster at Pharsalus he fled to Caesar for refuge. The second was Gaius Cassius, who [after Pharsalus] had surrendered his triremes to Caesar in the Hellespont. Both had belonged to Pompey's party. There was also Decimus Brutus Albinus, one of Caesar's dearest friends. Caesar always regarded them all as worthy of honor and trust, and he placed affairs of the greatest importance in their hands — for example, when he went off to the war in Africa he put them in charge of the armies in Gaul, Decimus in Transalpine Gaul, Marcus Brutus in Cisalpine. . . .

Talk of kingship grew ever louder and, as the senate was scheduled to meet before long, Cassius, gripping Brutus tightly, asked him, "What will we do in the senate house if Caesar's flunkies introduce a bill on kingship?" Brutus replied that he would not be present in the senate house. "But," continued Cassius, "what if we are summoned there as praetors — what will we do then, my dear Brutus?" "I will defend my country to the death," he replied. Cassius embraced him, saying, "Not one of the nobles will fail to join you if that is your intention. Do you think it is artisans and shopkeepers who have been writing those anonymous messages on your tribunal? No, it is the noblest of the Romans — men who expect horse races and combats of wild beasts from other praetors, but from you they expect liberty, your ancestral task."

That is when they first disclosed to each other what they had been turning over in their minds separately for a long time now. Next each proceeded to sound out his own friends and even some of Caesar's — the ones in each group whom they knew to be the most intrepid. Of their own friends they lined up the two brothers Caecilius and Bucolianus, and after them Rubrius Ruga, Quintus Ligarius, Marcus Spurius, Servilius Galba, Sextius Naso and Pontius Aquila; of Caesar's friends, Decimus Brutus, about whom I have spoken above, Gaius Casca, Trebonius, Tillius Cimber and Minucius Basilus.

When they thought they had enough and judged it unwise to reveal the plot to any more, they made a compact with one another, without oaths or sacrificial rites, and even so no one changed his mind or betrayed the secret. Then they looked for a time and place. Time was pressing because Caesar was to leave in four days on his campaign [against Parthia], and from then on he would have a military guard around him. As the place they were thinking of the senate house, in the expectation that the senators, even though uninformed in advance, would join them eagerly when they saw the deed — as is supposed to have happened when Romulus changed from king to tyrant.

They thought that their deed, performed like the one of old openly in the senate house, would be regarded as carried out not from a private conspiracy but for the good of the city and in the public interest, and would therefore not risk reprisals from Caesar's army. Moreover [even after the rest of the senators joined them], the honor of the deed would remain theirs, since everyone would know that they had been the leaders.

For these reasons they chose the senate house, and in this they were unanimous. But there was disagreement over ways and means. Some, for example, wanted to finish off Antony also, since he was consul with Caesar, his most powerful friend, and the one best known to the soldiers. But Brutus said that with Caesar alone could they earn fame as tyrannicides, since they would be killing a king, but if they killed his friends as well they would be regarded as Pompeian partisans venting their private hates. And the others were persuaded by this reasoning.

Now they waited for the senate meeting, which was imminent. The day before that meeting Caesar, taking along Decimus Brutus Albinus as a drinking companion, went to dine at the house of Lepidus, his master of horse. Over drinks Caesar proposed a discussion of "What is the best death for man?" Various preferences were expressed, but of all present he alone recommended an unexpected one. So he was, in effect, prophesying for himself, conversing about what was really to happen the next day. That night as he was drinking he fell into a stupor, and his wife Calpurnia had a dream in which she saw him covered with copious streams of blood. She tried [in the morning] to stop him from going out, and when he offered sacrifices the signs were repeatedly frightening. He was about to send Antony to dismiss the senate when Decimus arrived and persuaded him, in order to avoid being accused of contempt for the senate, to go in person to dismiss it. And so he went, conveyed in a litter.

As there was a spectacle on in Pompey's theater the meeting of the senate was going to be held in one of the rooms nearby, as was customary when the theater was thus occupied. Brutus and Cassius had come early in the morning to the portico in front of the theater and were conducting with complete impassivity the business incumbent upon them as praetors, but when they learned of Caesar's unfavorable omens and his postponement of the senate meeting the conspirators were thoroughly discomposed. While they were in such agitation a man took Casca by the hand and said, "You kept it secret from me, though I am your friend, but Brutus has told me the news." Casca, taken unawares, was confounded at the thought of his knowing, but the man continued with a smile, "And where, pray, will you get the money for an aedileship?" And Casca recovered himself. So too Brutus and Cassius, as they were conferring anxiously, were drawn aside by one of the senators, Popilius Laenas, who told them that he joined them in praying for what they had in mind and advised them to make haste. They were confounded, unable to say a word in their consternation.

Caesar had already left the house and was being borne to the meeting when one of his friends, having learned of the plot, came running to disclose what he had learned. He went into the house but, as he had not found out what was going on down to the last detail, he told Calpurnia only that he had need of Caesar on pressing matters and waited around for him to return from the senate house. Artemidorus, who had been Caesar's host in Cnidus, actually ran to the senate house but Caesar was already dying when he arrived. Still another man handed Caesar a rolled-up note about the plot as he was sacrificing in front of the senate house just before going in, and it was found in his hand after his death. Just as Caesar stepped out of the litter, Laenas, who a little before had joined his prayers with the Cassius group, rushed up and engaged him privately in earnest conversation. The conspirators were terrified at the sight of this lengthy encounter, and they nodded to one another that they would make away with themselves before submitting to arrest. But as the talk continued and they saw that Laenas did not look like a man informing but rather like one begging and entreating about something, they recovered themselves; and when they saw him conclude the conversation with a kiss, they took heart again.

It is the custom for magistrates entering the senate to

take the auspices before going in. Here again the omens were unfavorable. Caesar's first animal was without a heart (or, according to others, the top of the viscera was missing). The seer said this was a sign of death, but Caesar laughed and said the same thing had happened to him in Spain in his war against Pompey. The seer replied that he had been in extreme peril then and that now the sign was even more indicative of death. Caesar ordered to sacrifice again, but even so no propitious sign was vouchsafed. Reluctant to keep the senate cooling its heels, and egged on by his enemies pretending to be his friends, he disregarded the omens and went in. For what had to happen to Caesar had to happen.

One of the conspirators, Trebonius, was left behind to delay Antony in conversation in front of the door. After Caesar took his place of honor they surrounded his chair like friends — but they had daggers concealed. One of them, Tillius Cimber, came around in front and petitioned for the return of his brother, who was in exile. When Caesar kept dismissing and refusing it, Cimber seized his purple robe as though still entreating, and then he pulled it away, drawing it down to the neck and shouting, "Friends, what are you waiting for?" Casca, who was standing over Caesar's head, drove his dagger at his neck but missed and stabbed him in the chest. Caesar snatched his toga away from Cimber, grabbed Casca's hand, leapt down from his chair and, turning around, pulled Casca with tremendous force. But while he was doing that someone else drove a dagger into the side which was exposed as he turned. Cassius struck him in the face, Brutus wounded him on the thigh, Bucolianus in the back. With rage and shouts Caesar turned, like a wild animal, upon each of them, but after Brutus' blow he at last gave up, covered his head with his toga and fell with dignity by the statue of Pompey. Even so they continued to rain blows upon the fallen body, to a total of twenty-three wounds. And many of them wounded one another as they wielded their daggers.

Dio Cassius, *Roman History*, Book 44, chapters 1-19 [selections]

As Caesar was making the preparations for his campaign

against the Parthians, an accursed madness fell upon a group of men so that, envying him for overreaching them and hating him for being honored above them, they lawlessly slew him. In so doing they they introduced a new pretext for unholy infamy, scattered legislative acts to the winds, and plunged the Romans once again from concord into party strife and civil war. They, of course, claimed in slaying Caesar to be liberators of the people, but in truth they plotted against him impiously and threw the city into party strife when it was finally enjoying good government. Democracy has a fair name and appears to offer something like an equal share to all through equal rights, but in its acts it is proved to conform not at all to its appellation. In contrast, monarchy has a loathsome sound, but it is most fortunate to be a citizen under it because it is easier to find one good ruler than many. If finding even one strikes some as difficult, then the alternative must be admitted to be absolutely impossible, for it is not in the nature of many to acquire virtue. And even if a bad man should attain sole rule, he is still preferable to a mass of such, as is pretty well proved by the history of the Greeks and the barbarians, and indeed of the Romans themselves. . . . Under a democracy it is impossible for so large a city as Rome (so powerful and wealthy to boot) to adopt sound policies, and still more impossible to enjoy concord without such. If Marcus Brutus and Gaius Cassius had realized this, they would never have killed the city's ruler and protector; but by their act they became the cause of countless ills to themselves and to the whole contemporary world.

This is how it came about, and the cause of his death was the following. He had aroused resentment, which was not totally undeserved except to the extent that the senators were responsible. For it was they who first raised him up and puffed him up with novel and excessive honors, and then blamed him and slandered him because of those very honors, observing how gladly he had accepted them and that his manners were more offensive as a result of them. Caesar did occasionally err in accepting some of what they voted him, and in believing he really deserved it all. Nevertheless, the greatest fault lay with them because, after at first honoring him as he deserved, they then led him on

77

into culpability by the things they voted. As for him, he neither went so far as to refuse all of them which might appear contemptuous, nor could he safely accept them all: excessive honors and citations render even completely sound men a little conceited, especially if such laudations appear to be offered sincerely. . . .

When they began conferring honors upon him they assumed he would show some moderation. But as they went on and saw that he delighted in their awards . . . men competed with one another in proposing ever more exaggerated honors, some acting by way of flattery, others in mockery. Thus, some went so far as to authorize him to have intercourse with as many women as he wished, because even then, though in his fifties, he still had many mistresses. Others, and these were the majority, did it with the purpose of making him as quickly as possible a focus of envy and indignation, so that he might the sooner be slain — which is exactly what happened. Because of these very measures Caesar became confident that he would never be plotted against either by men who voted such honors or by anyone else with their aid. As a result he even dispensed with his bodyguard, that is, he accepted the concept that he was being watched over by the senators and equites, and disbanded his guard.

On one occasion honors more numerous and greater than usual were decreed by unanimous vote, except for Cassius and a few others (who thereby became notorious but suffered no harm — a striking display of Caesar's magnanimity). Then, they approached him as he sat in the vestibule of the temple of Venus, to tell him of their decrees, for they used to conduct such business in his absence, to give the appearance of acting not under duress but voluntarily. And he, whether through some divine disfavor or through an excess of joy, remained seated when receiving them. He thereby aroused in them all — not just in the senators but in the onlookers as well — such profound wrath as to provide his slayers with one of the chief pretexts for their conspiracy. Later some tried to excuse Caesar's conduct by saying that he had had an attack of diarrhea and was having trouble controlling his bowels, and that is why he remained seated — to avoid peristalsis.

But that did not convince most people, because not long afterwards he got up and walked home. So they suspected him of being overproud and they hated him for being haughty, when it was they who had made him arrogant by their exaggerated honors. And against the background of this kind of incident he later increased suspicion further by allowing himself to be designated dictator for life.

To the conspirators this was the last straw. They hesitated no longer, but, in order to render him odious even to his best friends, they circulated various slanders about him and climaxed them by addressing him as king, an epithet by which they had often referred to him among themselves. He kept rejecting the title and gently chiding those who called him by it, but he did nothing that would make anyone believe that he was truly annoyed by the appellation. Then they secretly crowned his statue on the rostra with a diadem, and when the tribunes Gaius Epidius Marullus and Lucius Caesetius Flavus removed it he became exceedingly angry, even though they made no disparaging remarks but, on the contrary, went so far as to praise him before the people as a man who wanted nothing of the sort. For a while, although vexed, he did nothing. Later, when some again called him king as he was riding to Rome from the Alban hills, he said his name was Caesar not King. But when those tribunes actually indicted the man who had been the first so to address him, then he could no longer restrain his wrath. . . .

Another such event, which occurred not long after the above, gave further indication that while he pretended to spurn the title, in reality he was eager to assume it. At the festival of Lupercal [on February 15th], after he had entered the forum and was seated on the rostra on a gilded chair, adorned in regal garb and resplendent in a garland interwoven with gold, Mark Antony, accompanied by his fellow priests, hailed Caesar as king and placed a crown on his head, saying "This the people give you through me." Caesar replied, "Jupiter alone is king of the Romans," and sent the crown to [Jupiter's temple on] the Capitol. But he showed no anger, and he had it recorded in the minutes that he had not accepted the kingship when it was offered him by the people through the consul. So the suspicion arose that the scene had been staged, that he did desire the title but wanted to be compelled somehow to assume it, and the hatred against him flared to new heights.

After this . . . Marcus Brutus and other men of spirit were approached privately and even provoked publicly. Numerous leaflets were broadcast exploiting his homonymity with the Brutus who overthrew the Tarquins . . . and maintaining the pretense [of such ancestry] in order that Marcus Brutus, in the guise of kinsman, might be stirred to comparable feats. They continually kept calling him to action, shouting, "O Brutus, Brutus," and adding "We need a Brutus." Finally, they wrote on the statue of the Brutus of old "Would that you were living!" and on the tribunal at which the present Brutus, as praetor, presided "You are asleep, O Brutus" and "You are no Brutus."

These, then, were the incidents that convinced Brutus to make the attempt on Caesar's life. He had, it will be recalled, fought against him from the start (but Caesar had subsequently been his benefactor), and he was both nephew and son-in-law of Cato called Uticensis. His wife, Portia, is said to have been the only woman who was privy to the conspiracy. . . .

Next he was joined by his sister's husband, Gaius Cassius, who had also been spared by Caesar and also honored with a praetorship. They then went about rounding up others who were likeminded, and their number was considerable. I certainly do not need to list the names of all the others — which would make tiresome reading — but I cannot omit the names of Trebonius and Decimus Brutus (who was also called Junius and Albinus). Caesar had been their constant benefactor, and Decimus had even been designated consul for the following year and assigned Hither Gaul[44] as his province, yet they joined in the conspiracy against him.

They were nearly discovered, what with so many people privy to the plot; but Caesar would not hear a word about anything of the sort, and reproved very severely those who brought any such reports. For another thing, they kept postponing: as it was they stood in awe of him, and in addition they were afraid that, even though he no longer had any guard, they might be killed by the others who were always around him. And that is what would have happened if they had not been forced, against their will, to hasten the attempt. For a story of the kind that are always being concocted had spread, whether true or false, that the priests called The Fifteen[45] were putting it about that the Sibyl had said that the Parthians could not be conquered except by a king, and that The Fifteen were therefore going to propose that that title be given to Caesar. The conspirators believed the rumor to be true and realized that when a decree of such importance was proposed to the magistrates, among whom were Brutus and Cassius, they could neither dare to speak against it nor endure to be silent. They therefore accelerated their plot before anything could be done about the decree.

They decided to make the attack in the senate. Caesar, they reckoned, would least suspect any danger there and would thus be overpowered more easily. Also, it would be safe and easy to have their swords carried into the chamber concealed in document cases, and the rest of those present, being unarmed naturally, would be unable to offer resistance. And if anyone should be so rash, they expected they would be helped by the large number of gladiators they intended to station in advance in the nearby theater of Pompey on the pretext of putting on a show there.

When the appointed day came they gathered in the senate house at dawn and sent word inviting Caesar to come. As for him, he received advance warning of the plot from soothsayers, and also from dreams. The night before he was slain his wife dreamed that their house had collapsed in ruins, and that her husband had been wounded by some men and had taken refuge in her bosom, and Caesar dreamed that he was raised aloft onto the clouds, where he clasped the hand of Jupiter. In addition omens neither few nor insignificant came to him. The arms of Mars, by ancient custom stored in his house as high priest, made a great noise during the night, and the doors of the room in which he slept opened by themselves. The sacrifices which he performed on account of these omens gave no favorable indication, and the birds he used in divination would not sanction his leaving the house. After his murder at least, some also regarded the incident of his gilded chair as ominous, that is the fact that, as Caesar tarried, the attendant carried the chair out of the senate house, thinking it would not be needed.

For the above reasons Caesar was so long in coming that a rumor spread to the effect that he would remain at home that day, and the conspirators became afraid that there would be a postponement and their plot would fall through and they themselves be exposed. They therefore sent Decimus Brutus, as one supposed to be a completely devoted friend of his, to get him to come. Decimus poohpoohed the reasons adduced by Caesar, and told him the senate was very eager to see him. Caesar was thus persuaded to set forth. At this, a bust of him that stood in the vestibule fell of its own accord and was shattered. But being destined to lose his life that day, he neither paid this any heed nor did he listen to a man who tried to inform him of the plot. That man handed him a papyrus roll in which all the preparations for the attack were accurately described, but he did not read it, thinking it contained nothing urgent. In short, he felt so confident that he turned to the soothsayer who had once warned him to beware that very day, and said in jest, "Where are your prophecies now? You see, do you not, that the day you feared is at hand and I am still living." The soothsayer is said to have said only this by way of reply, "Yes, it is at hand, but it is not yet past."

When he finally arrived at the senate house, Trebonius delayed Mark Antony somewhere outside. They had planned to kill both him and Lepidus, but they were afraid that if they destroyed a large number they might be vilified as having slain Caesar to attain supreme power for themselves and not to liberate the city as they claimed. They therefore decided to keep Antony away from the slaying of Caesar, and Lepidus was already in the suburbs, setting out on a campaign. So Trebonius talked with Antony, and at the same time the others gathered round Caesar, who was at his most accessible and affable. Some engaged him in conversation, others presented petitions, in order that he might be not the least bit suspicious. At the opportune moment one of them came up to him as if to offer some thanks, and pulled his toga down from his shoulder, thus giving the signal agreed upon by the conspirators. Then

82

they fell upon him from every side and stabbed him all together. Because of their large number Caesar could say nothing and do nothing, but veiled his face and was slain with many wounds. This is the truest version, but some add that he said to Brutus, as he struck a fierce blow, "Thou too, my son?"

Caesar the God

In the lands of the eastern Mediterranean divinity was from earliest times an attribute inherent in monarchy, and the successors of the native rulers — first the Hellenistic kings, then some conquering generals of the Roman republic and later the Roman emperors — were there celebrated in similar terms. In Italy, where deification before death was repugnant, or at least alien, to Roman tradition, the eastern pattern made its first appearance with Caesar. Some weeks before the assassination the senate, now heavily packed with his new appointees, decreed a whole series of unprecedented honors "and finally they addressed him explicitly as Jupiter Julius, and they decreed that a temple be dedicated to him and his Clemency" (Dio Cassius Book 44 chapter 6). In Appian's version (Book 2 section 106) "they decreed the creation of many temples to him as a god, and one jointly to him and Clemency, represented clasping hands."

During the years between Pharsalus and the Ides of March honorary statues to Caesar were erected everywhere, in large cities and small towns, and especially in those through which he passed on his various campaigns. The statue bases carried inscriptions of which the following constitute a representative sample.

Sylloge Inscriptionum Graecarum, 3d ed., no. 760
Ephesus, 48 B.C.
The cities in [the province of] Asia and the peoples and nations [honor] Gaius Julius Caesar son of Gaius, pontifex maximus, imperator, twice consul, god manifest descended from Mars and Venus, and universal savior of human life.

Ibid., no. 759
Copies found both at Athens and at Megara, 47 B.C.
The people [honor] Gaius Julius Caesar, pontifex maximus and dictator, their savior and benefactor.

83

Année épigraphique 1947, no. 55.
Late 45 or early 44 B.C.
The Roman citizens doing business at Cos [honor] the Coan community for their devotion to Gaius Julius Caesar, pontifex maximus, father of his country, and god.

Inscriptiones Latinae Selectae, nos. 72 and 73.
Probably early 44 B.C.
To the genius of divine Julius, father of his country, whom the senate and people of Rome have added to the number of the gods.

To divine Julius [this statue] has been erected by order of the Roman people under the law of Rufrenus.[46]

Caesar the Man

Suetonius, *Life of the Deified Julius Caesar*, chapters 45, 55-57

He is generally described as having been tall, fair-complexioned, shapely of limb, and rather full in the face with lively dark eyes. He enjoyed good health, except that toward the end he was subject to fainting spells and nightmares. Twice during his campaigns he suffered epileptic fits. He was rather fastidious in the care of his person: haircutting and shaving had to be done just so and, according to some detractors, he had excess hair plucked out. He was also chagrined by his baldness, which often turned up as the butt of jokes by disparagers. That is why he adopted the habit of combing what hair he had left forward from the crown of his head, and of all the honors voted him by senate and people there was none he received and made use of more gladly than the privilege of wearing a laurel wreath at all times and places. They say he was also a fancy dresser: he wore his purple-striped senatorial tunic with fringes down to the wrist, and was never without a girdle — a rather loose one, to be sure — over it. That was the point of Sulla's remark warning the *optimates* to watch out for that young fellow with the ill-fitting girdle. . . .

In oratorical as in military skill he either equalled or surpassed the fame of the most famous. . . . Listing the orators in his *Brutus*, Cicero says he sees no one to whom Caesar must take second place, and describes his manner of address as elegant, brilliant, and even magnificent and noble to a degree. In writing to Cornelius Nepos Cicero also said the following about Caesar: "Tell me, which of the orators that devoted themselves to nothing else would you place above him? Who uses epigram more pointedly or more often? Who is more distinguished or more elegant in his phrasing?". . . . His public delivery, they say, was in a high-pitched voice, with impassioned but not unattractive movements and gestures. A few of his speeches are extant, but some are of uncertain attribution. Augustus thought — not without good reason — that his *Defense of Quintus Metellus* must have been taken down by stenographers who had trouble keeping up with him as he spoke — even the title, I find, [is inexact] in some copies. . . .

There are extant also his *Memoirs* of the Gallic war and of the civil war with Pompey. The author of the books on the Alexandrian, African and Spanish wars is uncertain; some think it was Oppius, others Hirtius (the latter also completed the last, unfinished book of the Gallic war). Regarding Caesar's *Memoirs* Cicero remarks, again in his *Brutus*: "He wrote *Memoirs* which deserve the highest esteem. They are simple, direct and elegant, stripped, as if it were a garment, of all rhetorical ornament. But while his intention was to supply others with material to draw upon for the writing of history . . . , he has in fact [by his stylistic excellence] discouraged sensible men from doing so." Of those same *Memoirs* Hirtius boasts, "They are so highly esteemed in the general consensus that it looks as if historians have been robbed of an opportunity instead of being provided with one. Our admiration, moreover, is greater than that of the rest of the world, for everyone knows how well and perfectly he composed them, but you[47] and I know how easily and quickly he did it." In Asinius Pollio's opinion they were composed carelessly and with something less than the strict truth, because Caesar generally accepted accounts of others' deeds with uncritical credence, and also published — whether by design or through lapse of memory — inaccurate accounts of his own, but Pollio thinks Caesar was going to rewrite and correct all that. Also extant are his *On Analogy*, in two books, also two *Rebuttals of Cato* and a poem entitled *The Road*. He wrote the first of these while crossing the Alps on his way back to his army from holding assizes in Hither Gaul, the second about the time of the battle of Munda, and the third in the course of the twenty-four days it took him to get from Rome to Farther Spain. Also preserved are some letters of his to the senate, and he was, it appears, the first to send these in the notebook form of a memoir instead of sprawled across papyrus rolls as consuls and generals did before that. Letters to Cicero are also preserved,[48] and likewise letters to friends about domestic matters. In the latter, when he had something confidential to communicate, he wrote it in cipher, that is with the sequence of letters so arranged that no word could be made out. If you want to decipher and read those, change every letter of the alphabet to the fourth ahead of it, i.e. write *d* for *a*, etc. . . . .

He was highly skilled in arms and horsemanship, and his powers of endurance were beyond belief. On the march he was always at the head of his troops, sometimes riding, sometimes on foot, bareheaded rain or shine. He completed very long stretches with incredible speed, as much as a hundred miles a day, traveling light in a rented carriage, and if rivers got in the way he crossed them by swimming or on inflated animal-skins, so that he often got to the destination before the couriers sent to announce his arrival.

Plutarch, *Life of Caesar*, chapter 69 [in part]
Caesar died at the age of 56, surviving Pompey by not much more than four years. All his life he ran such great risks pursuing, and finally attaining, power and rule, but he reaped from them no fruit but only the name and an invidious fame among the citizens. Still, his great *genius* that had watched over him all his life followed him after death as an avenger of his murder, driving and tracking down his slayers over land and sea till no one of them was left, and pursuing any who had had a hand in the deed or participated in the plot.

Suetonius, *Life of the Deified Julius Caesar*, chapters 88-89

He died in his fifty-sixth year, and he was added to the number of the gods not only by a vote of the senate but also in the attitude of the masses. At the first performance of the games which his heir Augustus instituted to celebrate his deification, a comet appeared and continued to shine for seven days, rising about an hour before sunset. This was believed to be Caesar's soul, received into heaven; and that is why his statues have a star set on the top of his head.

The senate decreed that the hall in which he was cut down be walled up, that the Ides of March be named Parricide Day, and that no meeting of the senate ever be held on that day.

Practically none of the assassins survived him by as much as three years, nor died a natural death. Condemned one and all, they died in various ways, some in shipwreck, others in battle, and some took their own lives with the very same dagger with which they had stabbed Caesar.

III

THE VENGEANCE

From the Ides to Philippi
(44-42 BC)

We all swore to be guards of his person
or avengers of his death.
— Appian, *Civil Wars* ii.17.124

When think you that the sword goes up again?
Never, till Caesar's three and thirty wounds
Be well avenged.
— Shakespeare, *Julius Caesar* v.1

The tyranny lives, though the tyrant be fallen.
— Cicero, *Letters to Atticus* xiv.9

8

Wherefore Rejoice?

Cicero, *Correspondence with Friends* **Book 6, no. 15**
Though undated, this brief note — a mere nineteen words in
Latin — is generally thought to be Cicero's explosion of joy in
the first flush of the news of the assassination. The addressee
was one of the assassins: see p. 73. [Appian] A year later he
was himself murdered by his slaves in retaliation for his bar-
barous, mutilating punishment of some of them.

[Rome, 15 March 44 B.C.]
Cicero to Basilus, greeting.
   I congratulate you! For myself, pure joy. I love you, I
protect your interests. I hope you return my love and will
let me know how you are and what goes on.

   As Z. Yavetz puts it so well, "The conspirators fell prey to
their own propaganda and failed to perceive that a passing mood
expressed in the reaction of a vociferous minority does not nec-
essarily correspond with the sentiments of the silent majority.
This false assumption aroused their hopes that Caesar's assassination would put an end to tyranny." In other words, where
the conspirators dug their own graves was not in believing their
own anti-Caesarian shibboleths, but in believing that the people
would believe them. In the crunch the people chose Caesar's
heir over the "liberty" of the optimates.

Plutarch, *Life of Brutus***, chapter 18**
When Caesar had thus been done to death, Brutus stepped
forward intending to speak in heartening tones and keep
the senate in session. But they made for the exit helter-
skelter, and there was a shoving and a tumult by the door

even though no one was after them or driving them. The conspirators had firmly decided to kill no one else, but to proclaim the restoration of liberty for all. Except for Brutus, all the conspirators, when they were planning their enterprise, were for killing Antony along with Caesar: he was, they pointed out, pro-monarchy and violent, he had made himself powerful through close association with soldiery, and now, on top of his natural swagger and great ambition, he had acquired the authority of the consulship, and as Caesar's colleague to boot. But Brutus put his foot down against any such plan, firmly insisting, in the first place, on justice, and in addition holding out the hope of Antony's changing sides. For he refused to abandon the notion that Antony, being clever and ambitious as well as enamored of fame, would, once Caesar was out of the way, be drawn to emulate their noble course and join them in restoring the liberty of the fatherland. So Antony was saved by Brutus, but in fear of the moment [after the assassination] he put on a commoner's garb and fled.

Now Brutus and his associates went up to the Capitol and, displaying their bloodied hands and naked daggers, exhorted the citizens to liberty. At first all was shouting and rushing about, which, coming on the heels of the calamity, made the confusion greater. But as no other murder followed and no seizure of property, the senators and many of the populace took heart and approached the men on the Capitol. When a multitude had assembled Brutus made a speech suited to the occasion and aimed at winning popular support. When the audience applauded and called out to them to come down [from the Capitol], the conspirators took heart and went down into the forum, the rest of them proceeding in a body by themselves, while Brutus, surrounded and accompanied by many prominent citizens, was escorted with great fanfare from the citadel and was placed on the rostra. At that sight the multitude, though a motley crowd and ready to riot, stopped in its tracks and waited in polite silence to see what would happen. When Brutus stepped forward, all gave quiet attention to his words. But when Cinna in his turn began to speak and to denounce Caesar, they made it clear that the conspirators' deed was not to the liking of all, breaking into

91

a rage and berating Cinna so bitterly that the conspirators withdrew once again to the Capitol.

Appian, *The Civil Wars*, Book 2, sections 118-120

When the murderers had carried out so great a pollution — since the crime was in a sacred place and against a man sacred and inviolable — immediately there was a general flight, both in the senate house and in the whole city, and several senators were trampled in the confusion, and a few even lost their lives. Many another citizen and foreigner also met death, not by design but, as happens in a civil disturbance, by the mistake of those into whose hands they fell. . . .

The theater, too, was emptied as people fled in consternation and fear, and the markets were looted. Everyone locked his doors and prepared to defend himself from the rooftop. Antony fortified his house, in the belief that the plot was against himself along with Caesar. Lepidus, the master of horse, who was in the forum when he learned what had happened, sped to the island in the river, where he had a legion of soldiers, then marched them to the Campus Martius so as to have them ready at hand for Antony's orders (for he accepted being in second place to Antony, who was a closer friend of Caesar's and his co-consul). As Antony and Lepidus thought it over, their impulse was to avenge the fate that Caesar had suffered, but they were afraid that the senate would favor the murderers, so they continued to await developments yet a while.

There had been no military guard around Caesar, who did not like bodyguards, but only the retinue of his office had accompanied him to the senate house, together with many magistrates and a large crowd of citizens and foreigners, of slaves and freedmen. All these had fled en masse, but three slaves, the only ones to stay behind, put the corpse on a litter and unsteadily, since they were only three, they carried home the man who a little earlier had been ruler of land and sea.

The slayers wanted to say something in the senate house, but as there was no one left, they wrapped their togas around their left forearms for shields and, holding aloft their bloody daggers, they ran about shouting that they had killed a king and tyrant. One of them carried a cap on the end of a spear, a symbol of liberty,[49] and they called for [the restoration of] the ancestral constitution, calling to mind Brutus of old and his confederates of those days against the kings of old. Along with them, brandishing daggers, ran others who had had no part in the deed but laid claim to the glory — men like Lentulus Spinther, Favonius, Aquinus, Dolabella, Murcus and Patiscus; but as it turned out, they did not share in the glory, but they did suffer the same punishment as the perpetrators.

But the people did not rush to answer their call, and that left them perplexed and fearful. They had confidence in the senate, which, though it had fled at first in ignorance and confusion, consisted of their own relatives and friends, men who, like themselves, had found the tyranny oppressive. But they viewed with apprehension both the populace and Caesar's veterans, many of whom were then in the city — some of them had just recently been discharged from the army and allotted lands, others had already been settled in colonies but had come to the city to escort Caesar as he left [for the Parthian war]. The conspirators also feared Lepidus and the army under his command in the city, and they also feared that Antony, in his capacity as consul, might ignore the senate, call on the support of the people alone, and work some terrible harm on them.

In this situation they rushed up to the Capitol with their gladiators,[50] and took counsel with one another. Their best plan, they decided, was to distribute bribes among the populace, in the hope that if some of them began to express approval of what had happened, the rest would join in, counting on liberty and yearning for [the restoration of] the republic. In their minds the populace was still genuinely Roman, such as they had been taught it was when under the Brutus of old it destroyed the monarchy. They did not realize that they were expecting two mutually exclusive opposites, namely that the people of their day would be lovers of liberty and their faithful hirelings at the same time. The latter were more ready at hand, since the republic had long been corrupt.

Cicero, *Correspondence with Friends*, Book 2, no. 1

Written a mere two days after the Ides of March, this letter reveals the baffled, almost panic-stricken quandary in which the conspirators found themselves when their cry of liberty did not automatically return the government to them, as they had expected it would. The temper of the people had turned so ugly that they remained cooped up in their homes, fearful of appearing in public.

[Rome, morning of 17 March 44 B.C.].
Decimus Brutus to his dear Marcus Brutus and Gaius Cassius, greeting.

Here is how we stand. Last evening Hirtius called on me at my house. Antony's intentions, as he detailed them, are the most wicked, naturally, and the most treacherous. He said he could not possibly give me my province, and he did not think any of us was safe at Rome, so aroused were the feelings of the soldiers and populace. I think you realize that both statements are false, and that the truth is what Hirtius pointed out, to wit, Antony is afraid that, if we obtained even moderate support for our claims to office, there would be no role for him in the government.

Caught in this pinch I decided to ask for free legations[51] for myself and the rest of us, so we could find some honorable reason for leaving Rome. This he promised he would arrange, but I'm not confident he will, since those fellows are so insolent and so set on getting us. And even if they do grant our request, what will happen not long after, I think, is that we will be declared public enemies and interdicted from water and fire.[52]

"What, then," you say, "do you advise?" I think we must bow to fortune, get out of Italy, migrate to Rhodes or somewhere else in the world. If there is a change for the better, we will return to Rome; if there is no great change, we will live in exile; if the worst happens, we will resort to our ultimate defense.[53]

At this point it may occur to one of you to ask why we should leave that as our last resort instead of trying something now. Because we have nothing with which to make a stand. We have only the armies of Sextus Pompey [in Spain] and Caecilius Bassus [in Syria]. I think they will be in stronger positions when this news about Caesar reaches them, and there will be time enough for us to join them when we know what their strength really is.

On behalf of you and Cassius I will make any deal you wish me to — in fact Hirtius insists that I do so. So please answer me soonest, as I have no doubt I will have Hirtius' response to my request before 10 o'clock this morning. And in your answer tell me also where we can meet, where you would like me to come.

After my last talk with Hirtius I decided to demand police protection while we are in Rome, but I doubt they will grant it, for it would make them very unpopular. But I thought I ought to omit no demand that I judge to be equitable.

Appian, *The Civil Wars*, Book 2, sections 135-148

[On March 17th, with Antony presiding,] the senate passed a decree providing that Caesar's murder should engender no prosecutions, but all his acts and decisions should be valid. . . . Next, the leaders of the colonists [i.e., Caesar's veterans] demanded a special decree regarding them, in addition to the general one already passed, guaranteeing their land allotments; and Antony, far from opposing it, threw a scare into the senate so that they passed it and also a companion decree regarding the veterans who were just going out to their colonies. The senate then adjourned and some gathered round Lucius Piso [Caesar's father-in-law], in whose keeping Caesar had deposited his will, and demanded that he not make the will public and not give the corpse a public funeral, because those actions might start another revolution. He refused, and they threatened to prosecute him for defrauding the state of such a huge estate which was really public property (they were hinting, obviously, at a new tyranny).[54]

Thereupon Piso called out at the top of his voice, demanding that the consuls reconvene the senate (the senators had not yet left). Then he said, "These men who talk of having destroyed a tyrant are already so many tyrants over us instead of just one. They want to prevent me from burying the pontifex maximus, they threaten me if I publish his will, and they want to confiscate his property, again on the ground that he was as tyrant. . . . His burial is in your hands, but his will is in mine, and I will never betray a trust unless someone kills me first." There was applause and expressions of indignation were heard from all sides, especially from those who hoped there would be something in the will for them, and it was voted that the will be read in public and that the man be given a public funeral. On that note the senate adjourned.

[Next Brutus and Cassius sent messengers to summon the people to the Capitol, and Brutus delivered a speech before those who came, justifying the assassination and attempting to placate the veterans.]

At daybreak the consuls summoned the people to an assembly and read out to them the senate's decrees [of the previous day]. . . . Then Caesar's will was produced for all to see, and the people immediately ordered it read. In it Caesar adopted as his son his sister's grandson Octavius, and he bequeathed his gardens as a park for the people and to the city-dwelling Romans he gave seventy-five Attic drachmas per man.[55] The people were stirred again to anger on thus finding out that the will was that of a man who loved his country, the same man they had previously heard charged with tyranny. And it seemed to them especially pitiful that Decimus Brutus, one of the murderers, was adopted as heir in the second degree. . . .

When Piso brought the corpse into the forum a countless multitude, bearing arms, rushed to surround it as a guard. With acclamations and abundant ceremony they placed it on the rostra. There followed prolonged wailing and keening, and the armed men beat on their shields. Little by little they were changing their minds about the amnesty [granted the assassins]. Seeing this development, Antony, who had been chosen to deliver the funeral oration as consul for a consul, friend for a friend, and relative for a relative (he was related to Caesar on his mother's side), seized this renewed opportunity and cunningly spoke as follows.

"The funeral eulogy of so great a man ought properly to come, O citizens, not from me, one person, but from his whole country. To make this oration yours and not just Antony's I will read all the honors that in his lifetime all of you — senate and people alike — voted him in admiration of his excellence." And he read, agitated and gloomy of mien, enunciating each word distinctly and pausing to emphasize especially those decrees in which they divinized him and declared him sacred, inviolable, father of his country, benefactor and unparalleled protector. At each of these appellations Antony, illustrating his words with action, turned his face toward Caesar's corpse and pointed to it with his hand, and at each he made some brief comment, a mixture of grief and indignation. For instance, where the decree said "father of his country," he added, "This was a testimonial of his clemency." And at "sacred and inviolable" and "anyone else who fled to him for refuge should also be unharmed," he added, "So no one who fled to him for refuge was harmed, but he himself, the man sacred and inviolable to you, was killed. And yet he had not, like a tyrant, seized these honors from you by force, in fact he did not even ask for them. We are obviously the exact opposite of free men if we give such honors to the unworthy, even unasked. But you, O trusty citizens, to defend us from any such charge of not being free men, you will pay such honor to him even now that he is dead."

Next he read the oaths they had all sworn to guard Caesar and Caesar's person with all their strength, and to condemn those who did not protect him should someone plot against him. At which Antony, raising his voice and stretching out his hand toward the Capitol, declared, "O Jupiter of our forefathers and ye other gods, I myself am ready to avenge him, as I swore and vowed. But as my [senatorial] peers think their decree [of amnesty] will be for the good of the state, I pray it will be so." At this, which was obviously aimed at them, there was a stir among the senators, but Antony quickly backtracked to soothe them, saying, "What has happened, O citizens, would appear to be the work not of any man but of some malign spirit. The crisis of our great dangers is immediately before us or already at hand, and we should therefore look to the present rather to the past. Otherwise we may be drawn back into our previous civil strife and all the nobility that our city still retains will be utterly destroyed. Let us, then, send forth this sacred man to join the blessed, as we chant over him the customary hymn and dirge."

After these words he drew up his toga like one inspired, girded himself to give his arms free play, and took up a theatrical stance by the bier. He bent down to it and straightened himself up, he celebrated Caesar as a heavenly divinity, raising his hands aloft in witness of his divine birth. Next, in a rapid-fire voice he recited Caesar's wars, battles, victories, all the nations he had added to Rome's empire, all the spoils he had sent home. Each of these were presented as a marvel, with repeated cries such as "This man alone has emerged unconquered from all the foes who fought him. And you alone," addressing the corpse, "have avenged the violence visited upon the fatherland three hundred years ago, casting at your feet the only savage tribes to storm Rome and set it aflame." After more such frenzied talk Antony dropped his voice from ringing to plaintive tones, mourned and wept for a friend who had suffered an unjust fate, and swore he would gladly give his own life in exchange for Caesar's.

Irresistibly carried away to a peak of emotion, he uncovered Caesar's body, put the toga on the end of a spear and waved it aloft, rent as it was by the stabs and crimsoned with the dictator's blood. At this the people like a chorus joined him in most sorrowful mourning, and as they grieved they became filled with anger. The funeral oration was followed by other dirges sung to Caesar by choruses according to ancestral custom, and his exploits were once again recited, and also his fate. At some point in the lamentations a voice pretending to be Caesar's spoke, listing by name all of his enemies whom he had spared and helped, and of the murderers themselves exclaiming in mock wonderment, "Spared I them to murder me?"[56] The people could bear it no longer. . . .

At this point, when they were already close to violent outburst, someone held up over the bier an image of Caesar made of wax (since the body, lying on its back on the bier, could not be seen). The image was rotated by some contrivance, so that everyone could see the twenty-three stabs so savagely inflicted on his face and whole body. The people could no longer bear this pitiful sight before their eyes. Still voicing their lamentations they girded themselves and went into action. They burned the senate house where

98

Caesar had been slain, and they ran about hunting the murderers, who had long since fled from the scene. They were so maniacal with rage and grief that when they ran into the tribune Cinna, because he bore the same name as the praetor Cinna who had harangued against Caesar, without stopping to hear a word about the homonymy, they tore him to pieces so savagely that no piece of him was found to bury. They carried fire to the houses of the other assassins but there they were fought off, and when the neighbors pleaded with them they agreed not to use fire but threatened to come back the next day with weapons.

The people returned to Caesar's bier (in this interval the murderers fled secretly from the city) and bore it like a holy object to the Capitol, intending to bury it in the temple and place it among the gods. But the priests would not allow it, and they set it down again in the forum, by the royal palace of the Romans of old. They piled up sticks, benches (of which there were lots in the forum) and anything else of the sort, on that they heaped the opulent ornaments of the procession, many also tossing on their crowns and other decorations for bravery. Then they set it on fire, and the people en masse stayed by the pyre all night. The spot was first marked by an altar, but now there is a temple to Caesar, who is reverenced with divine honors.

Suetonius, *Life of the Deified Julius Caesar*, chapters 82-84

The conspirators had intended, after killing him, to drag his body into the Tiber, confiscate his property, and rescind his acts, but they desisted through fear of the consul Mark Antony and the master of horse, Lepidus.

At the instance of his father-in-law, Lucius Piso, Caesar's will was opened in Antony's house and read aloud. (He had drawn it up the previous Ides of September near Labicum, and had entrusted it to the safekeeping of the chief Vestal Virgin.) According to Quintus Tubero,[57] from his first consulship to the outbreak of the civil war he regularly named Pompey his heir and read it aloud to the assembled soldiery. But in his final will he listed three heirs, his sister's grandsons: Gaius Octavius to receive three-quarters of his estate, Lucius Pinarius and Quintus Pedius to share the remaining one-quarter. At the end of the document he also adopted Gaius Octavius into his family, giving him his own name. He named several of his assassins among the guardians of his son, should one be born to him, and named Decimus Brutus among his heirs of second degree. To the people he bequeathed his gardens near the Tiber as a public park, and three hundred sesterces to each individual.

When the day of the funeral was announced, a pyre was erected in the Campus Martius near the tomb of Julia. On the rostra was placed a gilded shrine modeled on the temple of Venus the Procreatress [of the Julian house], and in it was a couch of ivory with coverlets of gold and purple, and at its head a monument draped with the clothes in which he was slain. People bringing presents, as it appeared that a whole day would not be long enough, were instructed to bring them to the Campus in any order and by any route they wished. In the course of the funeral games these words, chosen from Pacuvius' *Ordeal by Arms*, were sung to arouse pity and hatred for his assassination: "Spared I them to murder me?" — and also words of like import from Atilius' *Electra*.[58] In lieu of a eulogy the consul Antony had a herald read out the decree in which the senate had voted Caesar all divine and human honors simultaneously, and likewise the oath by which the senators had bound themselves all to guard the personal safety of this one man; he then added a very few words of his own.

The bier on the rostra was carried into the forum by magistrates and ex-magistrates. Part of the crowd were for burning it in the temple of Jupiter on the Capitol, another part were proposing the senate house, when suddenly two figures, armed with swords and brandishing pairs of darts, appeared and set fire to the bier with blazing torches.[59] Without delay the crowd of bystanders piled on dry twigs, judicial tribunals with their benches, and anything else that could be contributed. Next the musicians and actors stripped off their garments (ornaments of his triumphs which they had put on for the occasion), rent them to bits and flung them into the flames. Veteran legionnaires threw in the arms with which they had adorned themselves for the funeral. Many women, too, tossed in the jewelry they were wearing and their children's amulets and robes.

9

Enter Octavian

Velleius Paterculus, *History of Rome*,
Book 2, chapters 59-60

Then Caesar's will was opened. In it he adopted Gaius
Octavius, his sister Julia's grandson. . . . Caesar loved the
boy as his own. When eighteen years old Octavius accompanied Caesar on his Spanish campaign, and thereafter
Caesar kept him at his side, sharing the same lodgings and
riding in the same carriage; and he even appointed him,
though still only a boy, to the priestly office of *pontifex*.
When the war was concluded he sent him to pursue his
studies at Apollonia [in Illyria], his aim being to polish the
natural gifts of this remarkable young man with training
in the liberal arts, and then take him along as his companion in arms in the wars against the Getae and the
Parthians.

When Octavius received word of his uncle's assassination, the centurions of the legions stationed near Apollonia
offered him their own and their men's support, and Sal-
vidienus and Agrippa urged him to accept the offer. But
he headed posthaste for Rome, and it was at Brundisium
that he learned the details of the assassination and the
terms of the will. In his progress toward the city enormous
crowds of well-wishers came to greet him, and as he entered the city there was seen above his head the orb of the
sun encircled by the colors of the rainbow, as if placing a
crown on the head of a man soon to reach such great
heights.

His mother Atia and stepfather Philippus advised him
against accepting the name of Caesar, which would surely

be invidious, but the beneficent fates of the state and the world claimed this consolidater and preserver of the Roman nation. . . . Therefore his divine spirit spurned mere human advice, and he resolved to pursue the loftiest goals with their risks rather than lowly ones in safety. He chose to adhere to his uncle's — likewise Caesar's — expectations of him in preference to his stepfather's, and he repeated more than once that he would be lacking in reverence to think himself unworthy of the name of which Caesar had deemed him worthy.

Appian, *The Civil Wars*, Book 3, sections 11-13

[Near Brundisium] the precise details about the murder and the public mourning reached Octavius, and also copies of Caesar's will and the senate's decrees — all the more reason, thought some, for him to beware of Caesar's enemies, since he was now his son and heir, and they urged him to renounce the adoption along with the inheritance. But he thought that for him to do that and not avenge Caesar would be shameful. He went to Brundisium, first sending ahead to make sure the murderers had not set any trap for him. And when the army stationed there came to meet him and received him as Caesar's son, he took courage and offered sacrifice, and was immediately hailed as Caesar. It is the custom among the Romans for adopted sons to take the names of their adopters. Octavius accordingly changed completely his own name and his patronymic, and instead of Octavius son of Octavius he was ever after known as Caesar son of Caesar.

Straightway, in crowds and from all directions, a mass of men began collecting around him as Caesar's son, some out of friendship for Caesar, others being his freedmen and attendants, still others, in addition to those, being soldiers who were serving there in the transport of supplies and money to Macedonia or of other moneys and tribute from other peoples to Brundisium. Encouraged by the multitudes flocking to him and by the universal goodwill shown him, he journeyed to Rome, accompanied by a crowd which was substantial to begin with and grew in size every day, like a spring flood. In this crowd he felt proof against any open plot, but by the same token he was all the more fearful of a secret trap, since practically all those accompanying him were recent acquaintances. Not all of the cities along his route were equally for him, but Caesar's veterans, to whom land allotments had been distributed, flocked from their colonies to greet the young man. They mourned for Caesar, condemning Antony for doing nothing about such an abomination and offering to take vengeance themselves if someone would lead them. Octavian praised their spirit but dismissed them, saying that would have to be put aside for the present. . . .

When he reached the city his mother and Philippus and all the others who were concerned about him expressed their fears: about the senate's estrangement from Caesar, about the decree that no one was to be prosecuted for Caesar's murder, and about the contempt shown Octavian by Antony — who was then the dominant figure — in neither coming himself nor sending anyone to greet Caesar's son on his arrival. Octavian calmed these fears, saying that he would go in person to greet Antony, deferring as a younger man to an elder, a private citizen to a consul, and that he would treat the senate with suitable respect. . . . But for him to renounce the inheritance and adoption would be to fail in his duty to Caesar and to cheat the people of their legacy. . . . In conclusion he invoked Caesar, not as friend but as father, not as fellow-soldier but as imperator, not as one fallen by the law of war but as one sacrilegiously cut down in the senate house.

Cicero, *Letters to Atticus*, Book 14, no. 4
[Lanuvium, 10 April 44 B.C.]
You don't suppose I hear anything here? But I do imagine that you in Rome get something new every day. Things are coming to a head. If Matius talks the way he does, what do you suppose the others will think? As for me, I am distressed at our failure to restore the republican constitution along with liberty — something that's never happened in any state. It's terrifying how they [the Caesarians] talk and threaten. . . .

But whatever happens, the Ides of March are our consolation. Our *héros divins* accomplished most gloriously and magnificently all they could by themselves. The rest requires money and armies, and we have neither. . . .

Ibid., no. 5
[Astura, 11 April 44 B.C.]
. . . It's not a good sign if the legions have raised their ensigns and are coming from Gaul. What about those that were in Spain — won't they make the same demands? . . .

You see what our magistrates are like — if they can really be called magistrates. What you really see are the tyrant's henchmen in positions of command, you see his armies, you see his veterans on our flank — all *prêt à flamber*. But the men whom the whole world should have been guarding and glorifying, those men are only praised and admired, but remain cooped up in their houses. Still, they at all events are happy, but the state is wretched.

But I should like to know about Octavian's arrival — any rallying to his side, any suspicion of a *coup d'état*? I don't suppose so, but whatever happened I want to know. I write this as I leave Astura, on the 11th.

Ibid., no. 6
[Fundi, 12 April 44 B.C.]
I got your letter today, while at dinner. Well then, in the first place you are feeling better, and in addition you send better news. The news that the legions were coming was certainly unpleasant. As for Octavian, it's neither here nor there. . . . Antony's parley with our heroes is not unsatisfactory under the circumstances. All the same, nothing that's happened so far gives me any real joy except the Ides of March. . . .

What can be more intolerable for us than retaining the very things for which we hated Caesar? Are we even to have for the next two years the consuls and tribunes of the people that he designated? I don't see how I can possibly *faire la politique*. For nothing is so *inconvenant* as having the tyrannicides praised to the skies and the tyrant's acts enforced. But you see our consuls, you see our other magistrates (if they can be called magistrates), you see the apathy of our optimates. Here in the country towns people are jumping for joy. There are no words to describe how happy they are, how they flock to me, how eager they are to hear what I have to say about the state of affairs. And meantime, not a single peep out of the senate. *Nous faisons la politique* so well that we live in fear of the defeated.

I have written you this letter over dessert. More, and *plus franchement politique*, later. And you too write what you're doing and what's doing.

Ibid., no. 10
[Puteoli, 19 April 44 B.C.].

Has it really come to this? Was this the purpose of my Brutus and yours, that he should have to stay at Lanuvium, that Trebonius should have to detour by back roads to get to his province, that all of Caesar's actions, papers, words, promises and plans should have greater force than if he himself were alive? Do you remember how on the very first day [i.e., the Ides] on the Capitol I screamed for the praetors to summon the senate to the Capitol? Ye gods, what great steps could have been taken then, when all our optimates and also those who generally supported us were rejoicing, and the political gangsters were shattered! You put the blame on Bacchus Day.[60] What could have been accomplished then? By then we were long since finished. You remember how you shouted that our cause was done for if he had a public funeral? Yet he was even cremated in the forum, eulogized pitiably, and slaves and beggars were dispatched to attack our homes with firebrands. What next? They have the gall to say, "Are you against Caesar's wishes?" I cannot take that and suchlike, and so I'm thinking of *"terre pour terre,"*[60] but your country [Greece] is *trop venteux.* . . .

Octavian came to Naples on the 18th of April. Balbus, who met him there early the next morning, was at my villa in Cumae later the same day and told me that Octavian will accept that inheritance [from Caesar]. But then, as you write, he'll have a big *brouhaha* with Antony. . . .

Ibid., no. 11

[At or near Cumae, 21 April 44 B.C.].
Day before yesterday I sent you a longish letter; now to answer your last.

I wish to heaven Brutus were at Astura. You speak of the *outrage* of that gang [of Caesarians] in Rome. Did you expect otherwise? For my part I look for still worse to come. When I read about a speech calling Caesar "so great a man," "our most illustrious citizen," I see red. True, by now such talk is a joke. But look you, demagogic harangues have been common, so habitual that our great heroes — gods, really — will abide in eternal glory to be sure, but not without ill will and not even without peril. Still a great consolation to them is the knowledge that they performed the grandest and most glorious of deeds. But where is the consolation for us, who have seen our king slain but are still not free? Well, luck will decide all this, since reason does not rule. . . .

Balbus, Hirtius and Pansa are here with me. Octavius has just arrived — right next door, at Philippus' villa — and he defers to me completely.[62] Lentulus Spinther stays here today, and is off tomorrow early.

Ibid., no. 12

[Puteoli, 22 April 44 B.C.].
My dear Atticus, I begin to fear the Ides of March have brought us nothing but joy and the satisfaction of our hatred and resentment. What awful news I get from Rome! And the things I see here! *O fait admirable mais sans issue.*

You know how warmly I feel toward the people of Sicily, and what an honor I consider it to be their patron.[63] Caesar conferred many benefits upon them, and I was delighted, but there was certainly no thought of granting them Latin rights, although — well, never mind about that. But now, look you, Antony has posted (for a powerful bribe, obviously) a law which — he says — was enacted by the Dictator in the Assembly, making the Sicilians Roman citizens,[64] and there was never a mention of any such thing when Caesar was alive. . . .

Octavius is here with me, all respectful and friendly. His

attendants were calling him Caesar, but not Philippus, and certainly not I. I don't see how he can be a loyal citizen.[65] He is surrounded by too many who threaten death to our heroes, saying the present situation is intolerable. What do you think they will do when the boy[66] comes to Rome, where our Liberators are already unable to remain in safety? They will be forever famous, and they are happy of course in the consciousness of their great deed. But we, if I mistake me not, will be prostrated. . . .

Ibid., no. 14

[Puteoli, 27 April 44 B.C.].

You defend the Brutuses and Cassius as if I were criticizing them, men whom I can't praise enough. It was the faults in the state of affairs, not in the men, that I tabulated. For the tyrant has been done away with but the tyranny, as I see it, lives on. Things are being said and done that he would never have done. . . . We could not be slaves to Caesar the man, but we submit to his memoranda. On Bacchus Day[67] . . . when we had come to the senate meeting, were we free to speak our minds? Didn't we have to do everything possible to placate the veterans who stood by under arms while we were defenseless? . . . But let's not talk about what's past. Let us watch over those men with all our care and protection, and, as you advise, let us be satisfied with the Ides of March. That day surely gave our friends, those divine heroes, entree to heaven, but it has not restored liberty to the Roman people. Recall your own words. Don't you remember shouting that all was lost if Caesar had a public funeral? Wisely said, indeed. And so you see what has resulted from it.

You say that on June 1st Antony is going to introduce a bill about the provinces, assigning Gaul to himself and extending the tenure of both consuls. Will we be allowed to vote freely? If so I will rejoice in the restoration of liberty. If not, what will the change of masters at Rome have brought me except the joy of having beheld the just killing of a tyrant. . . .

The short letter that you wrote after the other pleased me no end, the one about Brutus' letters to Antony and to yourself. It seems possible that things may be better than they have been up to now. . . .

Ibid., nos. 20 and 21

Most of Cicero's letters, especially those to Atticus, intimate friend and financial adviser, combine personal matters and politics. The personal, mostly omitted in this volume, are illustrated in the following letters.

The first of these letters is also one of several in which Cicero mentions Cleopatra. In 46 B.C. she came to Rome with Caesarion, her infant son by Caesar, who installed the royal party in a mansion in park-like surroundings on the Janiculan hill. Her presence was much resented, especially by anti-Caesarians, and after Caesar's death she did not long delay in returning to Egypt. On 16 April Cicero wrote to Atticus, "The Queen has fled — I couldn't care less." And two months later he still found occasion to remark, "I see red every time I remember the arrogance of the Queen when she was staying in the gardens across the Tiber" [*Letters to Atticus* Book 14, no. 8 and 15, no. 15].

[Puteoli, 11 May 44 B.C.]

20.

I sailed from Pompeii to stay with our friend Lucullus yesterday. On landing I was handed your letter . . . of the 5th. From Lucullus I came to Puteoli today and received two letters you wrote at Lanuvium, one dated the 5th, the other the 9th. This, then, will answer all three.

First, thanks for everything you've done about my affairs, both in the matter of payment and in the Albius business. About your estate at Buthrotum [in Epirus] — Antony came to Misenum when I was in Pompeii, but he was gone before I learned of his arrival. . . . I am sorry to hear of Tertulla's miscarriage: we need to produce as many Cassiuses now as Brutuses. I hope it's true about the Queen and that "Caesar" child of hers.

That takes care of your first letter. Now I come to the second. About . . . Buthrotum we'll talk, as you say, when I get back. Thanks for tiding [my son] Marcus over. You think I am wrong in thinking that the fate of the republic depends on Brutus, but that's the literal truth: either it will cease to exist or it will be preserved by him — or them . . .

If only Brutus could address the people! If he can be in the city safely, we've won. . . .

I come to your third letter. I am happy that my letter pleased Brutus and Cassius, and I have written them so. You want me to turn Hirtius more to our side. Well, I'm doing my best, and what he says sounds very good, but he chums with Balbus (who, to be sure, also speaks fair). You'll see for yourself what to believe. I see you are very pleased with Dolabella — so am I, very much so. In Pompeii I rubbed shoulders with Pansa, and he convinced me that he thinks right and wants peace. It's plain to me that the Caesarians are looking for an excuse for resort to arms. I applaud Brutus and Cassius' edict. You ask me to start pondering what I think our friends should do, but plans depend on circumstances, which, as you can see, change by the hour. . . .

My nephew Quintus, you write, is Antony's good little right hand. Through him, then, we will easily get what we want. I am waiting to hear what kind of speech Octavius made if, as you thought likely, Lucius Antonius gave him a public platform.

I must stop, because Cassius' messenger is leaving in a minute. I'm going now to say hello to Pilia, then by boat to a banquet at Vestorius'. Much love to Attica.[68]

21.

Not many minutes after I sent you a letter by Cassius' messenger my own messenger arrived [from Rome] and, to my dismay, no letter from you. But I quickly guessed you were at Lanuvium. . . .

Right after Cassius' messenger left Balbus dropped in. Good gods, it's easy to see he's afraid of peace and quiet. You know what he's like, how uncommunicative, but even so he told me of Antony's plans: he's making the rounds, getting the veterans to swear they will support Caesar's enactments, and urging them to have their weapons ready and inspected every month by the local magistrates. Balbus also complained of his own unpopularity, and everything he said made him sound like Antony's man. If you ask me, he's a complete fake.

But I haven't the slightest doubt that it looks like war.

That famous deed was performed with virile courage but with puerile planning. Who could fail to see that an heir to the throne was left alive?[69] Could anything be stupider?

I wrote this, or rather I dictated it, over dessert at Vestorius'. Tomorrow I'm planning to dine at Hirtius', and I'll set about bringing the fellow over to the optimates. *Quelle folie!* There's not one of that bunch who's not afraid of peace and quiet. So I'd better see to my winged sandals — anything is better than being in a war. . . .

10

Jockeying for Position

Cicero, *Correspondence with Friends,*
Book 11, no. 2
[Lanuvium, late May 44 B.C.]
Brutus and Cassius, praetors, to Mark Antony, consul.

Were we not convinced of your good faith and good will towards us, we should not be writing you this letter. But as that is your disposition, you will surely receive our words in the best light.

We are informed that a great crowd of veterans has now converged on Rome, that it will be much greater by June 1st. It would not be like us to have any doubt or worry about you. But certainly, since we have put ourselves in your hands and following your advice have dismissed our local supporters . . . we deserve to be made privy to your plans, especially where they concern ourselves.

We therefore ask you to inform us of your attitude regarding us, and whether you think we will be safe [if we come to Rome] in the midst of such a throng of veterans. . . . Events have made it clear that our aim from the very beginning was peace, and that we have sought no goal except freedom for all. No one but you can trick us — and that is alien to your honor and good faith. But no one else has the power to entrap us, for we have trusted and will continue to trust you alone. Our friends feel the greatest fear for us: although they have every confidence in your good faith, it nevertheless occurs to them that anyone can incite the crowd of veterans to any course of action more easily than you can hold them back.

We request that you reply to all our points. It is obviously silly and nonsensical to say the veterans were told [to descend on Rome] because you were going in June to introduce a bill about their rewards. Who do you think is going to stand in the way [of the bill], when we have agreed to do nothing? But no one should think us too greedy of life, because nothing can happen to us without general disaster and chaos.

Cicero, *Letters to Atticus,* Book 15, no. 12
[At or near Astura, ca. 10 June 44 B.C.]

. . . Octavian, I see, has no lack of intelligence or spirit, and he leaves the impression that his attitude toward our *héros* would be such as we would wish. But the big question is how far we can trust him, given his youth, his name, his inheritance, his *formation*. His stepfather, at least, thinks not at all — I saw him at Astura. Still, we must humor him and, if nothing else, detach him from Antony. . . . Moreover, he didn't seem to have much faith in Pansa and Hirtius.[70] Good instinct, *si cela dure.*

Cicero, *Correspondence with Friends,* Book 11, no. 3
[Naples, 4 August 44 B.C.]

Brutus and Cassius, praetors, to Mark Antony, consul.

We trust you are well. We have read your letter, and it is just like your edict — insulting, threatening, most unworthy of being sent to us. We have done you no injury, Antony, and we did not imagine you would be amazed if, in our capacity as praetors and men of standing, we issued an edict making a demand upon a consul. But if you *are* indignant at our having ventured to do so, then allow us to feel aggrieved at your refusing to grant even that to a Brutus and a Cassius.

As to the conscription of soldiers, exaction of moneys, deployment of armies and dispatch of couriers overseas — to all this you say you have made no complaint, and we of course believe you have acted with the best of intentions. But we deny any such actions, and we are surprised that you, although saying nothing on that score, have not been able to refrain from angrily hurling Caesar's death in our teeth. Consider yourself how intolerable it is for praetors not to be allowed to give up their prerogatives in the interest of harmony and freedom without the consul threatening them with armed violence for issuing such an edict.

Your reliance upon arms does not frighten us one whit: it neither beseems nor behooves us to humble our spirits before any danger, and Antony must not expect to give orders to those through whose efforts he is a free man. If other considerations impelled us to want to start a civil war, your letter would not stop us, for threats have no weight with free men. But you know full well that we cannot be pushed around, so perhaps you resort to threats in this matter so that we may appear to act out of fear rather than deliberation. This is our firm resolve: we are more than willing for you to be a great and honorable figure in a free republic and we seek no quarrel with you, but we value our freedom more than your friendship. Consider again and again what you are undertaking and whether you can stay the course, and reflect not on how long Caesar lived but on how short a time he reigned. We pray the gods that your designs may be for your own good and that of the republic, but if not, our wish is for the republic to be safe and honorable, with as little harm as possible to yourself.

"The funeral oration of Mark Antony had achieved its aim, and Shakespeare has transmuted it into a possession for all time; but Gaius Matius left a tribute to the memory of Caesar, which, although it is at present known only to the few who are versed in Latin literature, may eventually be recognized as of greater worth. Matius had offended the assassins and their sympathizers by helping to defray the cost of the games which Caesar had instituted in connexion with the foundation of the temple of Venus; and Cicero had made remarks about this and other matters which were repeated to Matius and wounded him" [T.R. Holmes, *The Roman Republic* III, p. 349]. Their exchange of letters follows, Cicero's apology to Matius and the latter's reply, generously accepting Cicero's "explanation" but refusing to repudiate his friendship for Caesar.

114

Cicero, *Correspondence with Friends*, Book 11, nos. 27 and 28

[Tusculum, late August 44 B.C.]
Marcus Cicero to Gaius Matius, greeting.

. . . Trebatius came to see me this morning, and when I asked him what's new he told me about your grievance [against me], and before I speak to that I want to set down a few words of preface.

As far back as I can remember, I have no older friend than you. And while the length of our friendship is something shared with many, the warmth is not. I took to you the day I met you, and I got the impression that the attachment was mutual. The subsequent differences in our lives — your departure and long absence, and my involvement in politics at Rome — prevented our predisposition toward each other from being cemented by habitual contact. Nevertheless I had proof of your affection for me many years before the civil war: when Caesar was in Gaul you arranged it, since you thought it was to my great advantage and not without advantage to Caesar, so he held me in esteem, cultivated me, and numbered me among his friends.

I pass over the many very friendly communications that passed between us in those days in conversations and letters, for more serious events followed. At the start of the civil war, on your way to Caesar in Brundisium, you called on me at my villa in Formiae. In the first place, how much that very fact meant, especially in those days! Furthermore, do you think I have forgotten the advice you gave, your conversation, your sympathy? . . .

There followed the time when I set out to join Pompey, driven by my sense of honor or duty, or by fortune — who knows? What service or effort did you begrudge, in my absence, in my interest or that of my family who remained behind? Was there anyone they all regarded as a better friend to me and to themselves. [After Pharsalus] I returned to Brundisium. Do you think I have forgotten how quickly you flew from Tarentum to my side as soon as you heard? how you sat by me and spoke, cheered me up, shattered as I was by fear of universal disasters? At long last we began to be together at Rome. Could any friendship have been closer than ours? In the most important matters I

115

could rely on your advice as to how I should conduct myself with Caesar, and in all other matters I had your good offices. Except for Caesar, was there anyone besides me to whom you paid the compliment of such frequent visits at home, so many hours spent in the pleasantest conversation? It was then too, if you remember, that you persuaded me to write these recent philosophical works. After Caesar's return [from Spain] was anything of greater concern to you than that I should be in closest friendship with him? And you accomplished it.

What is the point, then, of this reminiscence, longer than I intended? Why, because I was surprised that you, who should certainly know all this, would believe that I had done anything false to our friendship. . . . I admire everything about you, but above all your absolute loyalty as a friend, your counsel, dignity and constancy, to say nothing of your charm, urbanity and literary taste.

Which brings me back to your grievance. When I heard you had voted for that law,[71] my first reaction was not to believe it. Besides, even if I had believed it, I should not imagine you had done it without some valid reason. Because of your distinguished position nothing you do goes unobserved, and men's spitefulness often interprets your actions more adversely than they warrant. If you never hear such remarks, I don't know what to say. For my part, any time I hear one I defend you with the same spirit that I know you always defend me against my enemies. My defense, in fact, is bipartite: there are some allegations that I simply deny flatly, for example concerning this vote of yours; in other cases I defend you as acting out of of duty and sympathy, for example when you directed the games.[72] It does not escape a man of your keen intelligence that if Caesar was a king, as I certainly think, then one of two arguments can be applied to your performing that service — either, as I always insist, that you are to be praised for your loyalty and humanity in prizing a friend even after his death, or, as some others insist, that the liberty of the fatherland comes before the life of a friend. I only wish the arguments I used in such discussions had been reported to you, two especially, for which you deserve the highest praise — who brings them up more readily or more

116

often than I? — that you were the strongest voice first against starting the civil war and then for moderation in victory. I have found no one who does not agree with that.

And so I am grateful to Trebatius for giving me the occasion for this letter. If what I have written does not convince you, then you will have judged me wanting in all loyalty and sympathy, than which nothing can be more painful to me and more unlike you.

[Rome, end of August 44 B.C.]
Gaius Matius to Cicero, greeting.

Your letter gave me great pleasure, because I learned that your opinion of me is what I had hoped and prayed for. Although I had no doubt about that opinion, still, as I value it most highly, I was concerned to keep it intact. I was, moreover, satisfied in my own mind that I had done nothing that could hurt the feelings of a solid citizen. Accordingly, I was the less inclined to believe that a man of your many excellent qualities could have been induced to jump to any conclusion, especially a man toward whom my warmest good will has been and remains constant. Now that I know this is as I wished, I shall answer the charges which you have repeatedly rebuffed on my behalf, as was to be expected in view of your outstanding kindness and our friendship.

I know the charges that have been made against me since Caesar's death. People blame me for voicing grief at the death of a dear friend and expressing my indignation that a man I loved has been killed. They say that country must come before friendship, as if they had actually proved that his death has been good for the republic. I will not try to be clever — I confess I have not attained such heights of philosophy. I was not a partisan of Caesar in the political controversy, but I would not abandon a friend however much I disapproved of what he was doing. Nor did I ever approve of the civil war or even of the motive for the quarrel; in fact I did my utmost to have it nipped in the bud. And so, when my friend was victorious I was not seduced by the sweets of office or money — prizes which others, though they had less influence with him than I, clutched at with unrestrained avidity. On the contrary, my

117

own property was actually curtailed by Caesar's law [on debts], thanks to which most of those who are now exulting in his death were able to maintain their position in the state. I worked just as hard to have my defeated countrymen spared as I did for my own safety.

Can I, then, who wanted them all spared, help being outraged that the man who granted that boon has been killed? Especially as the same men were responsible for his unpopularity and his death? "You shall smart, then," they say, "for daring to condemn what we have done." What unheard-of insolence? Some men glory in crime, but others may not even deplore it with impunity! Why, even slaves have always been free to indulge their fears, joys and sorrows without anyone's dictation; but your "champions of liberty" are trying to wrest even that from us by their intimidating talk. But they will try in vain. No dread of danger shall ever turn me from conscience or from humanity. I have never thought an honorable death should be avoided; often it should even be welcomed. But why are they so angry with me for wanting them to be sorry for what they have done? I want everyone to feel grief at Caesar's death. Ah, but as a loyal citizen I ought to want to keep the republic safe. Well, if my life up to now and my hopes for the future do not prove — without my saying a word — that that is my earnest wish, I do not expect to convince them by talking.

I earnestly beg you, therefore, to judge by facts rather than words, and, if you think it important that right prevail, to believe that I can have nothing to do with scoundrels. Am I then, toward the end of my life, to change completely the principles I maintained in my youth, when I could have been excused any mistakes, and now undo the very texture of my life? I will not do it. Nor will I do anything to give offense, except that I do grieve at the harsh fate of a very dear friend and most illustrious man. But even if I were otherwise disposed, I should never deny any action of mine and thereby get the reputation of being a rogue in wrongdoing and a coward and hypocrite in concealing it.

Ah, but I directed the games given by the young Caesar in honor of the elder Caesar's victory! Well, that is a matter of private obligation that has nothing to do with the political situation. It was a service I was bound to render, after his death, to the memory and distinction of a very dear friend, and one I could not refuse when requested by a young man of excellent promise, entirely worthy of Caesar.

Also, I have often been to the house of Antony, the consul, to pay him my respects — and you will find that lots of those very men who proclaim me to be deficient in patriotism are continually going to him to ask for or get something. What insolence that is! Caesar never interfered with my associating with whomever I liked, even people he personally disliked; but these men, who have robbed me of a friend, try by their calumniation to prevent me from liking whom I like. But I am confident that the sobriety of my life will protect me in future against slander, and that even they, who hate me for my steadfast loyalty to Caesar, will prefer to have friends like me rather than like themselves.

As for me, if I get my wish I shall pass the rest of my life in retirement at Rhodes. If any accident intervenes to prevent that, I shall live at Rome, always desirous that right prevail.

Cicero, *Correspondence with Friends,* Book 12, no. 23

The reconciliation of Antony and Octavian was short-lived. By early October they were again at daggers' points — literally so, if there is anything to the charge Antony made that Octavian had suborned some of his bodyguards to assassinate him.

The addressee of this letter had been Caesar's quaestor in 48 B.C., his appointee as governor of Cilicia and Syria in 46 and 45, respectively, and at the time of this letter was governor of Africa. He also had some reputation as a poet.

[Rome, ca. 15 October 44 B.C.]
Cicero to Quintus Cornificius, greeting.
. . . I have no doubt that you receive detailed accounts of what goes on in the city. If I did not think so I should send you a full account myself, first and foremost of Octavian's attempt. On that subject the populace believes the charge was trumped up by Antony to give him an

119

excuse for making a raid on the young man's funds. But optimates and other realists both believe it and approve it. In short, there is great hope in him. There is nothing he may not be expected to do for public approval and glory. Our "dear friend" Antony, on the other hand, is so keenly aware of the great opprobrium in which he is held that, although he actually caught the assassins in his house, he will not risk publicizing it. On the 9th he set out for Brundisium to meet the four Macedonian legions, planning to win them over to his support with money so he can lead them to the city and tie them round our necks.

That's what the republic looks like today, if a republic can be said to exist in an armed camp. In that connection I am sorry you are too young ever to have had a taste of the republic when it was safe and sound. Up till now it was at least possible to hope [for a restoration], but now even that hope has been snatched away. . . .

Cicero, *Letters to Atticus*, Book 16, nos. 8 and 15
8.
[Puteoli, 2 or 3 November 44 B.C.]
When I know what day I'll be getting back I'll let you know. I have to wait for baggage to come from Anagnia, and there's sickness among my slaves.

On the evening of the 1st I got a letter from Octavian. He thinks big. He has won over the veterans at Casilinum and Calatia to his proposals. No wonder — he gives them 500 denarii apiece. He plans to make the round of the other military colonies. Obviously this points to his leading them in a war against Antony. And so I see that in a few days we will be under arms. But what sort of man are we to follow? Look at his name, look at his youth.

First he asks me [in his letter] for a secret parley, either at or not far from Capua. How naive if he thinks it can take place secretly. I wrote pointing out that it neither needed to be done nor was it possible. He sent me a friend of his, one Caecina of Volaterrae, to inform me that Antony is advancing on Rome with the Alauda legion, forcing the towns along the way to contribute money and marching the legion in battle alert. Octavian wanted my advice on whether to set out for Rome with 3,000 veterans, or hold

Capua and prevent Antony's passage, or go to the three Macedonian legions now marching along the Adriatic. He hopes these will be his because they refused to accept a donative from Antony — so he says, anyway — and they hurled fierce abuse at him and walked out on him as he addressed them. It's clear Octavian is offering himself as our leader, and he thinks I oughtn't withhold my support. I have, in fact, urged him to head for Rome. There, as I see it, he will have had the support both of the city rabble and also, if he inspires confidence, of the optimates. O Brutus where art thou? What a *bonne chance* you are missing! I certainly didn't predict precisely this, but I thought something of the sort would happen.

Now I ask your advice. Do I come to Rome or remain here or escape to Arpinum, a place that affords *sécurité*. Rome I suppose, lest it turn out that something good is accomplished and I am not there. Solve this one for me. I've never been in a greater *dilemme*.

15.

This is the last extant letter from Cicero to Atticus. "If others followed (and that is wellnigh certain), either Atticus prudently forebore to publish them, or the emperor on whose youthful intrigues they might have thrown a light too glaring, forebade their publication. Henceforth we must grope our way through the records of the dying Republic with less of Cicero's illuminating aid" [T.R. Holmes, *The Architect of the Roman Empire* I, p. 32].

At the time this letter was written Octavian was apparently still at Rome, but he left soon after and before the month was out Antony had followed, to counter Octavian's gains in Cisalpine Gaul. Cicero finally returned to Rome on the 9th of December, less than a fortnight after Antony's departure.

[Arpinum, ca. 15 November 44 B.C.]

. . . Many indeed are the words of wisdom I have heard from you on the subject of *la politique*, but none wiser than those in your last letter. Although at present that boy up there is pummeling Antony beautifully, nevertheless we had better await the outcome. What a speech he made! (A copy has been sent me.) "So may I attain my father's honors," he swears, pointing with outstretched arm to the statue. *Un tel sauveur n'est pas pour moi.*

But the clearest test, will be, I see, as you say, the tribunate of our Casca. On this very point, when Oppius was urging me to embrace the young man and his whole cause and band of veterans, I told him I couldn't possibly do so unless I were thoroughly satisfied that he would be not only no enemy to the tyrannicides but actually their friend. When Oppius said that's how it would be, I replied, "Then what's our hurry? He needs no help from me before the 1st of January, and before the Ides of December we will observe his disposition in the matter of Casca."[73] Oppius said he agreed completely. . . .

You say I had best stay in these parts till we hear how the present disturbances come out. That is wise and friendly advice. But, my dear Atticus, my trouble just now is not the republic — not that anything is or ought to be dearer to me, but even Hippocrates saw no use in prescribing medicine for hopeless cases. So let's forget all that. What weighs on my mind now is my finances, and not just finances but in fact my very reputation. . . . So come to Rome I must, right into the fire. Private bankruptcy is more dishonorable than public. . . . I have some thoughts on how to discharge my debts, but I can come to no decision before I see you. . . . Now you see what I'm worried about. So I'm coming.

Cicero, *Fifth Philippic*, sections 33-34, 42-53

On the first day of 43 B.C. the senate debated what course should be adopted with regard to Antony, who was still besieging Decimus Brutus in Mutina, while Octavian was now marching north to attack him. Some senators spoke in favor of sending Antony an ultimatum before declaring war on him. Cicero then delivered this oration, in which he decried all temporizing with a madman, and urged the senate to give Octavian its full backing against Antony. After a few more days of debate and political maneuvering Cicero's motion was passed.

I have been shown a letter sent by Antony to a member of the seven-man land commission, a gallows bird henchman of his. "Decide," he writes, "on what you desire, and what you desire you shall certainly have." There's the man for you, the man to whom we are urged to send envoys. . . . With that man, members of the senate, the issue can be decided only by war, war I say, and at once. Away with time-wasting embassies.

Therefore, to obviate the need for our passing more decrees every day, I move that the entire government be entrusted to the consuls and that they be charged to defend the republic and see to it that the republic suffer no harm.[74] And I further move that the men in the army of Mark Antony may leave him without prejudice if they do so before February 1st. If you pass these motions, members of the senate, you will in a short time recover the liberty of the Roman people and your own authority. Even if you follow a more gradual course, you will pass these same measures in the end, but by then it may be too late. . . .

I come now, members of the senate, to Octavian Caesar. Had he not appeared on the scene, who of us would still be alive? A man was speeding to Rome from Brundisium, a man totally without self-control, burning with hatred and hostility toward all loyal citizens, and leading an army. That man was Antony. What could we throw against his criminal recklessness? We had as yet no generals, no armed forces; there was no council of state, no liberty; our necks were exposed to his heinous savagery; we were all searching for a way to flee, and even flight afforded no escape.

What god then presented to us, to the Roman people, this divine young man? When every road to our destruction lay open to that pernicious Roman, suddenly and beyond all our hopes this young man appeared and, before anyone suspected that that is what he had in mind, he organized an army to oppose Antony's madness. Gnaeus Pompey received great honors while still a young man, and rightly so, for he came to the aid of the republic . . . yet he was much older and the soldiers were just looking for a leader. . . . Octavian Caesar, in contrast, is many years younger, and has fired veterans eager for retirement to take up arms again. . . . By his protection the tyranny of Antony has been crushed.

Therefore let us give Octavian the power of command, without which no military establishment can be run, no army held together, no war waged. Let him be a propraetor with the fullest powers of a regular incumbent. The office is great for one his youth, to be sure, but it serves our need for action as well as his career. . . . I now move as follows:

"WHEREAS Gaius Caesar [Octavian], son of Gaius, pontifex, propraetor, in this crisis of the republic has formed an army of veteran soldiers, rallying them to the liberty of the republic; and whereas the Martian and Fourth Legions, with the highest morale and singleminded in their exemplary defense of the republic under the command and authority of Gaius Caesar, are defending and have defended the republic and the liberty of the Roman people; and whereas Gaius Caesar, propraetor, has set out with an army for the relief of the province of [Cisalpine] Gaul, has brought horsemen, archers and elephants under his command and that of the Roman people, and at a most difficult time for the republic has brought succor to the lives and fortunes of the Roman people;

"NOW THEREFORE the senate decrees that Gaius Caesar, son of Gaius, pontifex, propraetor, shall be a member of the senate, sitting and speaking in the place reserved for praetors; and that for any office he may seek he shall be admitted to candidacy as would be legally permissible if he had been a quaestor the year before.[75]

. . . Those who envy young Caesar pretend they are afraid that he may not be able to restrain himself or act with moderation, that after being raised high by our honors he may use his powers too rashly. There is in fact no ground for such apprehension, for in the nature of things, members of the senate, a man who has grasped the meaning of true glory, who is aware that the senate and the Roman equites and the entire Roman people hold him dear as a citizen and as the salvation of the republic, such a man deems nothing comparable to such glory. Would that Gaius Caesar, I mean his father, had managed to endear himself so completely to the senate and all right-thinking citizens! But instead of pursuing that goal, he wasted all the power of his intellect, which was of the highest order, on the inconstant populace. And so, disregarding the senate and respectable citizens, he opened for himself that path to the enlargement of his powers which the spirit of a free people could not endure.

But his son is altogether different. He is most dear to all, including right-thinking citizens. On him our hope of liberty reposes, from him our safety has already been obtained, for him the highest honors are sought and prepared. When we are so full of admiration for his exceptional prudence, do we really fear that he will act foolishly? . . . I know all this young man's feelings inside out. Nothing is dearer to him than the republic, nothing more weighty than your authority, nothing more desirable than the good opinion of respectable men, nothing sweeter than true glory.

Therefore you not only have nothing to fear but ought even expect bigger and better things from him, and not fear that in him who has set forth to free Decimus Brutus from siege the memory of a family grief[76] will remain and carry more weight than the safety of the republic. I will even dare, members of the senate, something I should never dare to do without compelling reason — in fact I should fear getting a reputation for dangerous temerity. But I promise, I warrant, I guarantee, members of the senate, that Gaius Caesar [Octavian] will ever be the same good citizen he is today, ever such as we ought fervently wish and pray him to be. . . .

Moreover, concerning the army of Gaius Caesar I move that the following be decreed:

"The senate decrees as to the veteran soldiers who under the leadership of Caesar, pontifex, have defended and are defending the authority and liberty of the Roman people and the authority of this body, that they and their children shall enjoy exemption from military service;

"that the consuls, Gaius Pansa and Aulus Hirtius, either or both, shall at their pleasure determine what land there is, in the colonies in which the veteran soldiers have been settled, which is held in violation of the Julian law,[77] so that such land may be divided among the veteran soldiers; and they shall make a separate determination for the land in Campania,[78] and shall institute a plan for increasing the benefits to the veteran soldiers;

"that as to the Martian Legion and the Fourth Legion and those soldiers of the Second and Thirty-fifth Legions who came and enrolled under the consuls Gaius Pansa and Aulus Hirtius because the authority of the senate and the liberty of the Roman people was and is most dear to them,

125

that the senate decrees that they and their children shall enjoy exemption from military service except in case of an uprising in Gaul or Italy, and decrees further that these legions shall be honorably discharged immediately the war is finished, and decrees further that they shall be given the full amount of money promised to the soldiers of these legions per man by Gaius Caesar [Octavian], pontifex, propraetor;

"that the consuls, Gaius Pansa and Aulus Hirtius, either or both, shall at their pleasure make an inventory of the land that can be divided without injury to private individuals, and shall give and assign such land to these soldiers of the Martian Legion and the Fourth Legion to the fullest extent ever given and assigned to any soldiers."[79]

I have spoken, consuls, to all the proposals you have put before us. If these measures are passed quickly and without delay, you will quite easily make the preparations that time and the emergency demand. Speed is of the essence: had we employed it before, we should, as I have said repeatedly, be having no war now.

Cicero, *Tenth Philippic*, sections 25-26

In early March of 43 B.C. Marcus Brutus in Macedonia sent the senate a report on the state of affairs there. Upon receipt of the dispatch the consul Gaius Pansa raised in the senate the question of whether Brutus' fait accompli should be recognized by a grant of *de jure* authority over the provinces he in fact controlled. Cicero's Tenth Philippic was spoken in favor of the proposal, which the senate did in fact pass.

Under the circumstances, as to the proposal of the consul, Gaius Pansa, regarding the letter of Quintus Caepio Brutus,[80] proconsul, brought and read before this body, regarding that matter I move as follows:

"WEREAS by the effort, counsel, energy and valor of Quintus Caepio Brutus, proconsul, in a most difficult crisis of the republic the provinces of Macedonia and Illyricum and all of Greece and the legions and armies and cavalry units there are under the authority of the consuls, the senate and the Roman people;

"NOW THEREFORE [the senate decrees] that in so doing

Quintus Caepio Brutus, proconsul, has acted well and in the interests of the republic, and in keeping with his own and his ancestors' high station and with the customary practices of good government administration, and that his action is and will be welcome to the senate and Roman people;

"and let Quintus Caepio Brutus, proconsul, protect, defend, guard and keep safe the provinces of Macedonia, Illyricum and all of Greece; let him retain command of the army which he himself raised and constituted; let him, as need arises, collect and use for military purposes any public money that can be collected, and let him borrow money and requisition supplies for military purposes from whomever he sees fit; and let him make every effort to be as close to Italy as possible with his forces."

Cicero, *Eleventh Philippic*, sections 27-31

Toward the end of his consulship [44 B.C.] Dolabella went out to Syria, the province assigned to him to govern as proconsul. When passing through the province of Asia he surprised and killed Trebonius, the conspirator who had detained Antony at the door while Caesar was being assassinated inside the senate house. The news of Trebonius' death reached Rome soon after the senate had passed its decree legalizing Brutus' authority in Macedonia, and Cicero in the *Eleventh Philippic* proposed a similar authorization for Cassius in Syria. But the consul Pansa opposed the motion, and it failed of passage. Soon after, however, Cassius gained a *de facto* control of the area when Dolabella, besieged in Laodicea, killed himself rather than fall into Cassius' hands.

Did Brutus, since he knew our wishes, wait for us to pass decrees? No, he did not set out for Crete, the province assigned to him, but rushed to [Antony's] province, Macedonia. . . . He took over Dolabella's cavalry, convinced — even before Dolabella bloodied himself with this atrocious murder — that he was an enemy. Otherwise, by what right could he take over a consul's cavalry?

Again, take Gaius Cassius, a man endowed with greatness of mind and judgment equal to Brutus'. Did he not set out from Italy with the express purpose of keeping Dolabella out of Syria?[81] Under what law? By what right? Why, by that right which Jupiter himself has ordained, that everything conducive to the welfare of the state is considered legitimate and just: law, after all, is nothing but right reasoning derived from the will of the gods, prescribing what is permissible, forbidding the opposite. This, then, was the law Cassius obeyed when he set out for Syria, a province that belonged to another — or would belong, if men abided by the laws as written, but since these had in fact been trampled down it was his by the law of nature. But to confirm this also by your authority, I move:

"WHEREAS Publius Dolabella and those who were his agents, associates and abettors in a most cruel and most shocking crime have been judged by the senate to be enemies of the republic; and whereas the senate has decreed that a war is to be prosecuted against Publius Dolabella to the end that he — who has violated all divine and human law by a new, unheard-of and inexpiable enormity, and has committed himself to the execrable parricide of his fatherland — may pay to gods and men the penalties deserved and due;

"NOW THEREFORE the senate decrees that Gaius Cassius, proconsul, shall be governor of the province of Syria, like those who have been governors there with fullest title; that he shall take over the army from Quintus Marcius Crispus, proconsul, Lucius Statius Marcus, proconsul, and Aulus Allienus, legate, and they shall transfer command to him, and with those forces, and any others he may have collected, he shall pursue Publius Dolabella in war on land and sea. For the purpose of carrying on that war let him have the right and power to requisition from whomever he sees fit, in Syria, Asia, Bithynia and Pontus, ships, sailors, money and anything else related to carrying on that war; and in any province whatsoever into which he may penetrate for the purpose of carrying on that war, there let Gaius Cassius, proconsul, have greater authority than the man who shall then be governor of that province when Gaius Cassius, proconsul, comes into that province."

Cicero, *Correspondence with Marcus Brutus*, Book 1
No. 3

This letter was written in the euphoria occasioned by the news that in their first big battle, at Forum Gallorum near Mutina, Antony had been routed by the consuls Hirtius and Pansa, assisted by Octavian. Brutus at this time was at Dyrrhacium, in Epirus.

[Rome, 21 April 43 B.C.]
Cicero to Brutus, greeting.

Our situation seems much improved — you have, I know, been informed of what has happened. The consuls are seen to be the sort I repeatedly told you they were, and the boy Caesar shows a marvelous strain of nobility. If only we can guide and control him in the flush of his honors and popularity as easily as we have done till now! That will be altogether harder, but still I feel confident because the young man has been convinced, largely by me, that we owe our safety to him. All would surely have been lost if he had not drawn Antony off from the city. . . .

Yesterday I reaped the greatest fruit of my many efforts and sleepless nights (if solid and true glory can be said to yield fruit). A crowd as big as our city can contain rallied round me, escorted me all the way to the Capitol and then placed me on the rostra, to tumultuous cheers and applause. There is no vanity in me, indeed no reason why there should be, but still I am moved by the unanimity of all classes, their thanks and congratulations, because I find it a glorious thing to be the people's hero in their hour of preservation.

But I prefer that you hear about this from others. I should like you to inform me in detail about your doings and plans. And be especially careful that your graciousness not give the impression of laxity.[82] It is certainly the view of the senate, certainly of the Roman people, that no enemies have ever been more deserving of the supreme penalty than citizens who took up arms against the fatherland in this war. And whenever I speak in the senate I am for unrelenting retributive justice against all such, and all loyal citizens applaud. You must of course make up your own mind about this, but my view is that the case is one and the same against the three Antonius brothers.

129

No. 16

Although some scholars have sought to prove Nos. 16 and 17 spurious, the weight of scholarly opinion regards these letters as genuine messages from Brutus. The letters are full of self-righteous inflexibility in adherence to principle, expressed in a pompous and turgid rhetoric familiar to most people from Shakespeare, who captured it so well.

[Macedonia, May 43 B.C.]
Brutus to Cicero [in Rome], greeting.

I have read an extract from your letter to Octavius, which was sent me by Atticus. Your efforts and concern for my safety give me pleasure, though they are hardly news: repeatedly, indeed daily, do I hear about you that you have spoken or done something loyally and honorably in defense of my position.

But what you say about us in that same portion of your letter to Octavius has afflicted me with pain as great as my soul can contain. Has it really come to this, that you thank him in the name of the republic, and — must I say it? it is humiliating in one of our place and rank, but still I must say it — you so humbly and abjectly commend our safety to him? Such safety is more baneful than any death. You keep saying that the tyranny has not been destroyed, only the tyrant has been changed. Examine your words [to Octavian] and see if you can deny that those words of yours are the entreaties of an enslaved subject to a king. You say there that the one thing demanded and expected of him is that he consent to keep safe the citizens esteemed by our loyalists and the Roman people. And if he does not consent shall we not be safe? I had rather not be than be so by his charity. By heaven I do not think that the gods are all so hostile to the safety of the Roman people that we have to beg Octavius for the safety of any citizen, let alone for the liberators of the world — yes, I prefer, and it is certainly fitting, to speak proudly, especially to people who do not know where one's fears and goals ought to lie.

You admit, Cicero, that Octavius has so much power and you remain his friend? Or, if you hold me dear can you want me to appear at Rome when I can only do so with that boy's permission? Why do you thank him if you think he has to be asked to consent and allow us to be safe? Or must we consider it a benefit that he has preferred to be himself instead of acting like Antony, from whom we had to ask such favors? Is anyone addressing to the liberator from another's tyranny, instead of to its successor, the plea for those who have performed the greatest service to the republic to be allowed to live out their lives in safety?

The fault for such weakness and despair rests with the others as well as with you. That is what impelled Caesar to desire a kingship, induced Antony after his death to try to take the dead man's place, and now has so exalted that boy of yours that you judge he must be entreated to grant safety to men like us, and that we will be safe in no other way than through the mercy of one even now hardly a grown man. . . .

[We refused a deal with Antony because] we would not sell our principles and liberty at any price. Now this boy, whom the very name of Caesar seems to inflame against Caesar's executioners, what would he think it was worth, if there were any chance of a deal, to attain all the power he would have with our support if we were willing to settle for our lives, fortunes and the rank of consulars? But then he at whose death we rejoiced will have been killed in vain if we are going to be none the less his slaves even when he is dead. Doesn't this bother anyone? It does me, and the gods and goddesses can take everything from me but my firm determination not to stand for in his heir what I would not in him whom I killed — as I would not stand for it even in my father, should he come back to life — that is to let him be more powerful than the laws and the senate with my acquiescence. . . .

What have we done but fall back into the same prison if we beg him who has adopted the tyrant's name — I remind you that in the Greek city-states when tyrants are put down their sons suffer the same punishment — to allow the avengers and suppressors of the tyranny to live? Am I to be content with a state, or even regard it as a state, which cannot recover its ancestral and inculcated liberty, which has greater fear of a boy bearing the name of a slain king than confidence in itself, even though it sees how that very man who had the greatest power was slain by a

131

few men of courage? Henceforth commend me not to your Caesar, nor yourself either, if you take my advice. You must value exceedingly dearly what few years you can still expect at your age if for their sake you are going to kowtow to that boy of yours. . . .

It does not seem to have occurred to you that if Octavius is deserving of any honors at all because he waged war on Antony, then the service of those who excised the fundamental disease (of which today's situation is but a vestige) could never be adequately requited by the Roman people even if they heaped up together everything they have to bestow. . . .

To return to your strategy, I am the sort who not only will not be a suppliant but will even put down anyone who demands to be supplicated. Or else I will stay far away from willing slaves and in my mind Rome will be wherever I can be free, where I will pity your kind for whom the allure of living can be dimmed neither by your advanced age nor your accumulated honors nor the courageous example of others. As for me, I shall consider myself happy so long as I retain unswervingly and unceasingly the conviction that my patriotism has earned people's gratitude. For what is better than the memory of principled actions and, content with liberty, to disregard human vicissitudes? I will certainly not yield to yielders, and I will not be conquered by persons who are ready and willing to be conquered themselves, but I will make every effort and attempt, without letup, to rescue our country from slavery. If the outcome is as happy as it ought to be, why we shall all rejoice. If not, I will rejoice all the same, for on what actions or meditations can this life of mine be spent than on those that relate to liberating my fellow citizens?

I beg you, Cicero, and I exhort you not to grow weary or despair. Always, when warding off present evils, also look out for others that may creep in subsequently if they are not obviated. You realize that the brave spirit of freedom with which both when consul and now as a consular you have defended the republic is lost without constancy and imperturbability. . . . If the Cicero who acted with such great firmness and nobility in driving out Antony wavers in his judgment in regard to others, he will not only destroy any future fame but will even cause his past achievements to fade from sight. For nothing is inherently great unless there exists a basis for judging it so. Whether the basis be native ability or past achievements or devotion or popular demand, there is no one whom it more behooves than it does you to love the republic and be a champion of liberty. Therefore no more asking Octavius to consent to our being safe, but wake up and realize that the state in which you have performed the greatest services will be free and noble if only its people have leaders prepared to resist the plots of traitors.

No. 17

[Macedonia, May 43 B.C.]
Brutus to Atticus [in Rome], greeting.

You write me that Cicero wonders why I say nothing about his political activity. Since you put it to me directly, you force me to tell you what I think.

That Cicero has always acted with the best of intentions, that I know — is there anything of which I can be more certain than of his attitude toward the republic? But this most discreet of men, though he did not hesitate on behalf of the republic to take on Antony (then at the height of his power!) as an enemy, seems to me to have done certain things — how shall I put it? — unskilfully or with ulterior motive. I can only tell you this, that the boy's greed and wilfulness have been excited rather than abated by Cicero. . . .

Our Cicero boasts to me that he has conducted a war with Antony, though himself a civilian. What good does that do me if the price demanded [by Octavian] for crushing Antony is to take Antony's place, and if the protector [Cicero] against that evil [Antony] becomes the sponsor of a second evil [Octavian], and one that will, if we allow it, have deeper roots and foundation? Granted that those are the actions of a man afraid of tyranny or a tyrant. I, however, have no thanks for someone who, so long as his master is not ill-tempered, acquiesces in the condition of slavery itself. Even more, he [Octavian] is offered a triumph, and pay for his soldiers, and is encouraged by all sorts of decrees [of the senate] not to shrink from coveting the position of the man whose name he adopted. Is that worthy of a consular or of a Cicero? Since you have compelled me to break my silence, what you will read herein will unavoidably be disagreeable to you, and for my part it is with great pain that I write you this. . . .

Cicero, you say, is still apprehensive about the surviving remnants of the civil war. Can anyone be so apprehensive about a war that is practically over as to think there is nothing to be feared in the power of the victorious army's leader or in a boy's foolhardiness? Or is the reason for Cicero's action that he thinks the boy's stature is now so great that we must confer everything upon him without even being asked? O the enormous folly of fear, to be so on the watch against the thing you fear that you actually invite and attract it when you perhaps could have avoided it. We are too fearful of death, exile and poverty. No doubt these seem to Cicero to be the worst of evils, and as long as people from whom he can get what he wants, and who will make much of and flatter him, he does not reject servitude if it be but accompanied by respect — as if there could be any respect in what is the worst and most wretched degradation. Therefore, though Octavius call Cicero "father," consult him in everything, praise him, thank him, still it will be clear that his words are belied by the facts. For what is so alien to common sense as to regard as one's father a man who does not even count as a free man?[83] Nay the purpose, the aim, the outcome toward which this most worthy man is rushing is that Octavius be well-disposed to him.

For my part I set no store by those skills in which, I am aware, Cicero is the most accomplished man alive. What good to him now are his beautifully composed writings: the speeches on behalf of the liberty of the fatherland, the essays on dignity, death, exile, poverty? How much better those things are understood by Philippus, who puts less store by his stepson than Cicero does by this stranger! Therefore let him cease aggravating our troubles with his boasts. For what does it profit us that Antony is defeated if he is defeated in order to vacate for another the position he had held?

Your letter, to be sure, indicates that matters still hang in the balance. Since Cicero can do so let him indeed live submissive and servile, if neither his age nor his honors nor his achievements give him pause. As for me, there will never be any terms of servitude so good as to stop me from carrying on the fight against the condition [of political servitude] itself, that is against kingship and extraordinary commands and absolutism and any power that wants to be above the laws. . . .

It grieves me that you will be upset by this letter, since you are most devoted to all your friends and especially to Cicero. But assure yourself that my personal goodwill toward Cicero is not a whit decreased, but my opinion of him is, and in large measure. But that is as much as can be asked of any man, to judge each case as and how he sees it.

11

The Second Triumvirate and the Proscriptions

In the summer of 43 B.C. Octavian was master of the situation in Rome. He had himself and his cousin Quintus Pedius named to succeed the fallen consuls, and had laws passed confirming his adoption as Caesar's heir and outlawing the assassins. "The time had come for Octavian to consummate that formal reconciliation with Antony which he had long meditated, and, leaving Rome, he marched leisurely towards Cisalpine Gaul. Since Antony and Lepidus had combined, he must either join them or submit; and without the aid of Antony he could not punish Brutus and Cassius . . . Antony and Lepidus, strengthened by the accession of Pollio and Plancus, were far superior in force to Octavian, but they needed his assistance; they and their new allies were also Caesarians; and they knew that his soldiers were devoted to him. All was ready for an accommodation" — T. R. Holmes, *The Architect of the Roman Empire* I, pp. 68-69.

Appian, *The Civil Wars*, Book 4, sections 2-3

Near Mutina, on a lowlying islet in the river Lavinius,[84] Octavian and Antony moved together from enmity to friendship. Each had five legions of infantry. Leaving these stationed on the opposite banks, they proceeded with only three hundred men each to the bridges over the river. Lepidus in person went ahead, searched the island and waved his cloak for both to come. They left their three hundred on the bridges in charge of friends and advanced to the middle in plain view. Then the three held a council, Octavian sitting in the middle and presiding because he was consul. After two days of such conferencing from morning to night, they reached the following decisions: Octavian would resign the consulship and Ventidius[85] would

136

assume it for the rest of the year; a new magistracy, "for restoration from the civil wars,"[86] would be enacted for Lepidus, Antony and Octavian to exercise for five years with power equal to that of consuls (they decided to use that appellation rather than dictators, perhaps because of Antony's earlier decree outlawing any future dictatorship); the three then would at once designate the annual magistrates for the five-year period; and they would parcel out the provincial governorships among themselves, Antony obtaining the whole of Gaul except a strip called Old Gaul along the Pyrenees Mountains, Lepidus obtaining this together with Spain, and Octavian obtaining Africa, Sardinia, Sicily and the other islands there.

Thus the three divided the Roman empire among themselves, postponing the lands beyond the Adriatic because Brutus and Cassius still controlled those. Antony and Octavian, it was agreed, would carry the war to Brutus and Cassius, while Lepidus, consul the following year, would remain behind in the city to perform his duties there, and would govern Spain through deputies. Lepidus was to retain three of his legions for service at Rome, dividing the remaining seven between Octavian and Antony, three to the former and four to the latter, so that they would each march to war at the head of twenty legions. Now they boosted army morale with the prospect of war booty, with gifts, and especially with the allocation of eighteen Italian cities for military colonies. These were cities that were outstanding for their wealth, lands and buildings, and these were to be distributed to the army — lands and buildings alike — just like enemy country captured by force of arms. The most prominent of these cities were Capua, Rhegium, Venusia, Beneventum, Nuceria, Ariminum and Vibo. Thus they carved out the fairest parts of Italy for the army, and they also decided first to destroy their personal enemies, as a precaution against disruption while they were carrying out their plans and waging war abroad.

These were their decisions, which were reduced to writing in the form of an agreement, and which Octavian, as consul, then read aloud to the armies (omitting the list of the proscribed). The soldiers cheered what they heard, and they embraced one another in reconciliation.

Plutarch, *Life of Cicero*, chapter 46

Cicero had assisted Octavian in his bid for the consulship and delivered to him the senate's support. At the time he was criticized for this by his friends, and a little later he came to realize that he had ruined himself politically and betrayed the liberty of the people. For the young man, once he had obtained the consulship and increased his power, cast Cicero aside. He made friends with Antony and Lepidus, united his forces with theirs, and divided the sovereignty with them, just like any other piece of property. They also drew up a list of men to be put to death, more than two hundred of them. The longest wrangling in their bargaining came over the proscription of Cicero, Antony rejecting any deal unless Cicero was first on the death-list, Lepidus pitching in with Antony, and Caesar [Octavian] holding out against them both. For three days they met secretly, by themselves, near the city of Bononia, on an island in the river some distance from their armies. Caesar, it is said, fought for Cicero the first two days, then gave in on the third day and abandoned him. The *quid pro quo*'s were as follows: Caesar to give up Cicero, Lepidus his brother Paulus, and Antony his maternal uncle Lucius Caesar. Thus were they removed by rage and resentment from human considerations; or rather, thus did they reveal that no wild beast is more savage than man when he combines power with wrath.

Appian, *The Civil Wars*, Book 4, sections 5-11

When they were by themselves the three drew up a list of men to be put to death, singling out the powerful whom they viewed with suspicion, as well as their personal enemies. They even surrendered their own relatives and friends to each other for destruction, both then and also later; for others were repeatedly added to the list, some out of enmity, others for a simple offense or for being a friend of enemies or an enemy of friends, or because of exceptional wealth. They needed a lot of money for the war: Brutus and Cassius had appropriated and were still receiving the tribute of Asia collected by kings and governors, while they, with Europe and especially Italy exhausted by wars and exactions, were short of funds. Therefore they levied very heavy exactions on the citizenry, both men and women, and they planned to impose taxes on sales and rents. Now too, some persons were proscribed because they owned beautiful country or town houses. The total number of those condemned to death and confiscation was about 300 senators and close to 2,000 of those called equites. Among them were brothers and uncles of the proscribers, also a number of officers serving under them who had offended their superiors in some way.

Proceeding from their conference to Rome, they decided to hold off publicizing the bulk of the proscription list while they dispatched teams to take unawares and kill off first a dozen — some say seventeen — of the most important men, among them Cicero. Four of these were slain immediately, at dinner or in street encounters, and as the others were hunted or searched for in temples and houses, a sudden panic swept the city. The whole night long people were shouting and running about lamenting, as if in a captured city. For, with the realization that there was a manhunt on, and in the absence of any previously posted list of the condemned, every man thought he was being sought by the couriers. . . . The consul Pedius hurried about with heralds calling out to the people not to despair but to wait for morning to learn precise details. When morning came Pedius, contrary to the intentions of the triumvirs since he did not know what they had decided, posted the names of the seventeen as the only ones responsible for the civil misfortunes and the only ones condemned, and he gave the rest of the people public pledges of safety. Pedius died that night, worn out by his exertions.

The triumvirs entered the city on three successive days, each of them in turn, Octavian, Antony and Lepidus, each with his praetorian guard and one infantry legion. As they marched in the city was quickly filled with arms and ensigns distributed in strategic places. In their midst an assembly was at once convoked, and the tribune Publius Titius introduced a bill creating for a period of five years a new magistracy of triumvirs — Lepidus, Antony and Octavian — for settling the present disorders,[87] with power equal to that of consuls. . . . No interval was allowed for consideration and no future date fixed for voting,[88] but the law was passed forthwith. That night, in addition to the seventeen, the names of 130 other men were posted at many points in the city, and a little later another 150 names. And names were continually being added, of men subsequently condemned, or of men killed by mistake, to make it look as if they were rightly killed. It was ordered that the heads of all victims be brought to the triumvirs for a specified reward, consisting of money for a free man, freedom as well as money for a slave. All persons were required to open their homes to the search, and anyone who harbored or concealed a fugitive, or did not submit to the search, would be liable to the same penalties as the fugitive; while anyone who came forward to denounce any of these forbidden acts would receive the abovementioned rewards.

The edict of proscription reads as follows. "Marcus Lepidus, Marcus Antonius and Octavianus Caesar, elected to restore concord and order to the republic,[89] declare as follows: If treacherous cowards had not begged for mercy and after receiving it become enemies of and conspirators against their benefactors, then neither would Gaius Caesar have been killed by those whom he captured in war but then out of pity spared, made his friends and distinguished in large numbers with magistracies and offices and bounties, nor should we now be compelled to deal thus wholesale with those who, adding insult to injury, have proclaimed us public enemies. So now, seeing that the wickedness of those who killed Caesar and conspired against us is unresponsive to kindness, we prefer anticipating our enemies to being their victims. Surely no one who sees how Caesar and we have been treated can consider our action unjust or cruel or excessive. Behold Caesar, dictator, pontifex maximus, who subjugated and annexed as provinces nations most formidable to Rome, who was the first man to venture on the previously unsailed sea beyond the Pillars of Hercules, where he discovered a land unknown to the Romans, this was the man whom openly in the senate house, a place designated as sacred, before the faces of the gods, they slew with twenty-three savage wounds, these men whom he had captured in war and spared, even writing some of them into his will to be heirs of his estate.

The rest, instead of punishing those accursed for this abomination, sent them forth to magistracies and governorships, and they have used these offices to lay hold of the public monies, with which they are collecting an army against us and organizing a second army made up of barbarians ever hostile to our empire. Cities under Roman rule refusing to join them have been burned, razed, destroyed, and the others have been terrorized into joining them against the fatherland and us.

"Some of them we have punished already, and with divine assistance you will shortly see the rest paying the penalty. The biggest tasks — those in Spain, Gaul and here at home — have been dealt with and are under control, but there is still one left, viz. to march against the assassins of Caesar across the sea. As we prepare to engage in this struggle abroad on your behalf, we do not think it safe either for your interests or for ours to leave the rest of our enemies behind our rear to profit from our absence and watch for their chance in the fortunes of war. Neither do we think it safe, in so great a crisis, to tarry here because of them, but rather we must get rid of them completely, since it was they who started the war against us when they voted their decree declaring us and the armies under us to be public enemies.

"They, now, have doomed to destruction such countless numbers of citizens along with us; neither the retribution of the gods nor the opprobrium of mankind restrains them. We, on the other hand, shall deal harshly with no great multitude. We shall not name as enemies all who differed with us or even plotted against us, or any persons merely for reasons of wealth, affluence or high station, or so many as another dictator before us — him whom you called [Sulla] the Fortunate because of his successes — put to death when he too was bringing order to the city after civil wars, even though a triumvirate perforce has more enemies than one man. We shall punish only the vilest and guiltiest of them all. This we shall do for your sake no less than for our own, since the conflict between them and us must perforce place you all in great danger. Our army, which our common enemies have reviled, outraged and declared a public enemy, must have its satisfaction. We could have

141

seized all those we wanted at one fell swoop, but we prefer to proscribe rather than to seize them unawares, and this too we do for your sake, so that the enraged soldiers cannot take it upon themselves to multiply the victims by going after the innocent, but their targets will be numbered and designated by name and they will keep their hands off all others, as per our order.

"With good fortune be it then! No one is to receive, conceal, assist in flight or accept a bribe from anyone whose name appears in the list subjoined to this edict. Anyone discovered to have saved or helped or connived with any such, will himself be listed by us among the proscribed, with no excuses or pardons. Those who kill the proscribed are to bring in their heads, and for each head a free man will receive 25,000 Attic drachmas,[90] and a slave his personal freedom plus 10,000 Attic drachmas and the citizenship status of his ex-master. Informers will receive the same. To guarantee anonymity no written record will be kept of those receiving the rewards."

Such was the proscription edict of the triumvirs, as translated from Latin into Greek.

Dio Cassius, *Roman History*, Book 47, chapters 7-11

The murders were carried out mainly by Lepidus and Antony, who in the long time they had held magistracies and governorships under Julius Caesar had acquired many enemies. Octavian, it would seem, participated simply as their partner in power, since he himself felt no need at all to kill large numbers. He was not naturally cruel, having been brought up in his father's ways. In addition, as he was still a young man and had only recently entered politics, he was not under the great pressure of many violent hatreds, and he did want to be liked. A further indication is the fact that once he was freed from joint rule with them and held the power alone, he never again did anything of the sort. And even at that time he not only refrained from destroying as many as possible, but even saved very many, and he treated most harshly those who betrayed their masters or friends and most leniently those who helped others. Take the case of Tanusia, a woman of note, who at the outset concealed her husband Titus Vinius, one of the proscribed, in a chest in the house of one of his freedmen, Philopoemen by name. His disappearance thus gave the impression that he had been killed. Next she waited for a public festival that a kinsman of hers was to direct, and she arranged through his sister Octavia for Octavian to enter the theater alone, without the other two triumvirs. Thereupon she rushed in, informed him of what she had done (he had had no inkling), had the chest brought in, and from it produced her husband. Octavian expressed his admiration by releasing them all, even though death had been proclaimed for persons concealing any of the proscribed, and elevating Philopoemen to the rank of eques.

Octavian, as I was saying, saved the lives of as many as he could. Lepidus enabled his brother Paulus to escape to Miletus, and he was not inexorable toward the others. But Antony killed savagely and mercilessly, not only the proscribed but also those attempting to help any one of them. He would inspect the severed heads even if he happened to be at table, and he sated himself to the fullest extent on that most unholy and most pitiful sight. His wife Fulvia, too, caused the death of many out of personal enmity or for their money, in some cases men her husband did not even know — in one case, at least, when he saw the head he said, "I don't know this fellow." But when the head of Cicero, who was overtaken and slain while trying to flee, was brought to them, Antony first hurled floods of invective against it and in order that it might be seen — together with the right hand, which had also been cut off — then ordered it displayed on the rostra more prominently than the rest, in the very place where Cicero used to be heard attacking him. And Fulvia, before it was removed for display, took the head between her knees, opened the mouth, pulled out the tongue and stuck her hairpins in it, all the while jeering at it with a string of obscenities. Nevertheless even they saved some persons, those from whom they got more money alive than they could have hoped to obtain by their deaths, and where the removal of these names created blanks in the list they substituted other individuals. In fact, except for releasing his uncle at his mother's incessant entreaty, Antony performed no act of kindness.

143

Consequently the murders took many forms, and also the rescues of individuals were of many kinds. Many perished at the hands of their dearest friends, and many also were saved by their bitterest enemies. Some took their own lives, and others were set free by the very ones who had come to murder them. Some who betrayed masters or friends were punished, and others were honored for the same thing. Some who helped fugitives paid the penalty, others received rewards. For inasmuch as not one man was involved but three, each doing everything by his own desire and for his own private advantage . . . many complicated situations arose, according as they felt good will or hatred toward anyone. For my part, therefore, I shall not attempt to recount every case in precise detail — which would be an enormous task resulting in no great enhancement of my history — but I shall mention the cases I regard as most deserving to be remembered.

In one case a slave hid his master in a cave, but someone else played the informer. To save his master from imminent death he changed outer garments with him, and in that guise, as if he were really the master, he went forth to meet the attackers and was slain. Then they turned back, thinking they had murdered the one they were after, and when they had gone the master made his escape. In another similar case a slave changed his entire dress with his master, then sat himself in a covered litter and put his master to work as one of the carriers. Then, when they were overtaken he was murdered without even being looked at for identification, and the master by pretending to be a mere porter was saved. Now those slaves no doubt acted as they did to repay kind masters for some earlier benefaction. But there was even one branded slave who, so far from betraying the man who had had him branded,[91] threw himself heart and soul into saving him. As he was sneaking his master away somewhere their flight was discovered and a pursuit organized. Whereupon he killed a chance passerby, gave his clothes to his master, placed the corpse on a pyre and, taking his master's clothing and signet ring, went to meet the pursuers and pretended he had killed his master as he tried to escape. Seeing the spoils he carried and his brand marks, they believed him, and thus he both saved his master and earned honor for himself. Those are anonymous memorials. Then there was Hosidius Geta, whose son saved him by staging a funeral for him, as if he had died. And Quintus Cicero, the orator's brother, was hidden by his son, who did all he could to save him: he hid his father so well that he could not be found, and when subjected to every torture for it the son did not tell; but when the father learned what was happening, filled with admiration and pity for his son he voluntarily came out of hiding and gave himself up to his murderers.

Such were some of the outstanding acts of courage and filial devotion that were performed in those days. In contrast, Popilius Laenas killed Marcus Cicero even though Cicero was his benefactor, having once defended him; and to assure that he would not only be said but would also be seen to have done the murder, he erected a statue of himself garlanded beside Cicero's head, with an inscription recording both his name and his deed (and he thereby so pleased Antony that he got more money for his reward than the amount promised in the proclamation). Again, Marcus Terentius Varro was a man who never hurt a soul, but he had the same name as one of the proscribed and he was afraid that because of this he might suffer the same fate as Cinna; so he posted a notice — he was a tribune — to that effect and thereby became an object of sport and ridicule. Here is still another example of the uncertainty of life: Lucius Filuscius had previously been proscribed by Sulla but had survived; this time he was again put on the list and was killed, while Marcus Valerius Messala, though condemned to death by Antony, not only continued to live out his life in safety but was later appointed consul in place of Antony himself. [92]

The Death of Cicero

Plutarch, *Life of Cicero*, chapters 47-49

Cicero, with his brother Quintus, was at his country place near Tusculum. Learning of the proscriptions they decided to move down to Astura, an estate of Cicero's near the coast, and from there to sail to join Brutus in Macedonia (a report was abroad that he was in control there). . . .

[Quintus, who decided to go home, collect some possessions and then follow his brother, was killed.] Cicero was carried in his litter to Astura. . . . Then, after vacillating among many confused and contradictory plans, he put himself in the hands of his domestics to convey by sea to Caieta, where he had lands and a welcome retreat for the summer time, when the Etesian winds blow most pleasantly. The place also has a temple of Apollo, a little above the sea. A flock of crows arose from the temple and flew noisily to Cicero's boat as it was being rowed to land, and alighting on both sides of the yard-arm some cawed while others pecked at the rope ends. All agreed this was a bad omen, but Cicero landed, went to his villa, and lay down to rest. Most of the crows perched on his window, cawing uproariously, and one, flying down onto Cicero's couch as he lay completely covered, tried with its beak little by little to draw the cloak away from his face. The servants, seeing this and rebuking themselves for waiting around to be spectators of their master's murder . . . partly by entreaty and partly by force took him and carried him in his litter toward the sea.

Meanwhile, however, his murderers had arrived, Herennius a centurion and Popillius a tribune (who had once been defended by Cicero against a charge of parricide), and assistants. They broke in the doors, which they found barred, but Cicero was nowhere to be seen and those inside said they had no idea where he was. The story goes that . . . a freedman of Cicero's brother Quintus told the tribune Cicero's litter was being carred along the thickly wooded and closely shaded walks to the sea. The tribune took a few men with him and ran around the woods to the paths' exit, while Herennius dashed along the walks. When Cicero became aware of him he bade the servants stop and set down the litter. Then taking his chin in his left hand — a habit of his — he looked straight at his murderers. Squalid and shaggy, his face wasted with cares, he put his head and neck out of the litter and, while most present covered their faces, Herennius slew him. He died in his sixty-fourth year.[93] Herennius cut off his head and, by Antony's special instructions, the hands with which he had written the *Philippics*, the name which Cicero himself had given to his speeches against Antony and by which they are known to this day.

When Cicero's extremities were brought to Rome Antony happened to be conducting an election, but when he received word and saw them he cried out that now the proscriptions could come to an end. He ordered the head and hands to be placed on the rostra above the ships' beaks, a sight that horrified the Romans, to whom it seemed they were seeing not so much the face of Cicero as a reflection of the soul of Antony.

12

Philippi:
The Republic's Final Curtain

The Two Battles at Philippi: October-November 42 B.C.

Appian, *The Civil Wars*, Book 4, sections 108-138

Brutus and Cassius arrayed their forces on the higher ground and, in the hope of starving out their enemy, decided not to come down and force the battle. There were nineteen infantry legions on each side, those of Octavian and Antony being at full complement while those of Brutus and Cassius were short of that; but the latter had 20,000 cavalry, including Thracians, to the others' 13,000. Thus in numbers of men, in the boldness and bravery of the generals and in their arms and equipment, both sides afforded a most brilliant array.

For several days nothing happened. Brutus and Cassius did not want to engage, still hoping to wear down the enemy through supply shortages, since they themselves had a plentiful commissary all brought by sea from nearby Asia, while their enemy had no abundant supply they could count on. There was nothing that merchants could bring them from Egypt, which was drained dry by a famine in the land, nothing they could get from Spain or Africa on account of Sextus Pompey, nothing from Italy on account of Murcus and Domitius;[94] and Macedonia and Thessaly, the only areas then supplying them, would not last very long. With these calculations in mind Brutus and Cassius delayed as long as possible. But Antony, alarmed by these same calculations, decided to force them into battle. . . .

[After a preparatory manoeuver and a counter-move by Cassius] Antony made a daring uphill charge at an angle across the space between the two armies. This bravado provoked Brutus' troops into a bold oblique counter-charge . . . which they launched on their own, in advance of any order from their commanders. They killed all the men they encountered in this flank attack, and once they had begun the operation they also charged Octavian's army (which was drawn up right opposite them), routed them, pursued them to Antony and Octavian's joint camp, and captured it. Octavian himself was not in the camp, having been warned in a dream to beware of that day, as he himself informs us in his memoirs. . . .

Antony carried on his charge as he had begun it and, continuing uphill under a steady hail of missiles, he forced his way to Cassius' unit, which, guarding its assigned position, was stunned at his unexpected arrival. Boldly breaking through this unit he dashed to the wall that had been built between the marsh and the camp, demolished the palisade, filled in the ditch, undermined the fortification, slaughtered the men at the gates, withstood the missiles raining down from the wall, and ended by forcing his way in through the gates while some of his men got in at the undermined places and others by climbing up on the debris. All this happened so fast that the men who captured the fortification could turn to meet a contingent coming up from the marsh to help the defenders. While the main bodies of both sides battled outside, these men who had scaled the wall with Antony, unassisted, in a powerful charge drove the rescue party back into the marsh and returned to Cassius' camp. . . .

Cassius, when he had been driven from his fortifications and no longer had a camp to return to, hurried up the hill to Philippi to take stock of what was happening. While he could not see everything clearly on account of all the dust stirred up, he could see that his own camp alone was taken. Whereupon he ordered Pindarus his shield-bearer to fall upon him and kill him. As Pindarus delayed, a messenger ran up to say that Brutus was victorious on the other wing and was plundering the enemy camp. Cassius' only reply was, "Tell him for me, 'May you win a complete victory!' "

And turning to Pindarus he said, "What are you waiting for? Why don't you deliver me from my shame?" Then he offered his throat and Pindarus made away with his master. . . .

The end of Cassius' life occurred on his very birthday, on which, as it happened, the battle was fought. . . . Brutus wept over the corpse and called Cassius the last of the Romans, meaning that there would never again be another like him in nobility. . . .

On the same day as the battle at Philippi there also occurred the following great disaster on the Adriatic sea. On transport ships convoyed by a few triremes Domitius Calvinus was bringing to Octavian two infantry legions . . . as well as a praetorian cohort of some 2,000 men, four squadrons of cavalry and another body of picked troops. Murcus and Ahenobarbus met them with 130 warships. A few of the leading transports got away under sail, but then the wind suddenly failed and the rest, spread out over the sea, were caught in a dead calm and delivered by the gods into the hands of the enemy. . . .

The pressure on Octavian and Antony to take action was building, because the pinch of hunger was already being felt and was getting bigger and more frightening every day. They could not obtain sufficient supplies from Thessaly, and there was no hope of anything by sea, where the enemy fleet now held complete sway. . . .

But Brutus held to the same plan he had adopted at the start, all the more so when he learned about the hunger [in the enemy camp] and the success on the Adriatic, and saw the enemy's desperation resulting from lack of supplies. He preferred to withstand a siege or anything else rather than join battle with men driven desperate by hunger, with no hope or resource but in their own two hands. But his army, in their folly and impatience, did not agree. . . . His officers also kept after him with pleas to profit now from the army's high morale. . . . So Brutus, against his better judgment, finally led forth his army and arrayed them in line of battle before the camp wall. . . .

Both sides alike divined that this day, by this battle, would decide the fortunes of Rome once and for all. And it did.

The day was consumed in preparations till about three o'clock in the afternoon, when two eagles fell upon each other and fought in the space between the armies. There was the most complete silence. Then, when the eagle toward Brutus' side took flight, a piercing shout arose from the enemy and military standards on both sides were raised.[95] The onslaught was violent and savage. There was little call for the usual missiles of war — arrows, stones, javelins — because instead of resorting to the usual battle practices and tactics they closed in combat with naked swords, killing and being killed as they tried to break through each other's ranks. On one side they were fighting for their lives rather than victory, on the other for victory to convince their reluctant general. There was slaughter and groaning [of wounded] everywhere, and as their bodies were carried back out of the fray others from the reserves would take their places. The generals rushed everywhere, observing, cheering on their men, urging them on to ever greater exertions, relieving the exhausted so that there was always fresh courage in the front line.

Finally Octavian's soldiers, whether from their fear of famine or from Octavian's own good luck (for Brutus' men were certainly not at fault), began to move the enemy line. It was like turning a very heavy machine. They were being pushed back, back, step by step, but still in an orderly retreat. But they they broke ranks and gave ground more quickly, and the second and third lines of reserves retreated with them. In disorder now, all mingled together, they were hemmed in by one another and by the enemy, who pressed them without letup till it became an open rout. . . .

The next day Brutus, seeing [that the situation was hopeless] called to a friend of his, an Epirote named Straton, and asked to be stabbed. As Straton urged him to reconsider, he called to one of his slaves. Then Straton said, "Brutus, you shall not want for a friend rather than a slave to carry out your last bidding, if your mind is truly made up." So saying, he thrust his sword into the side of Brutus, who neither shrank nor turned away.

Thus died Cassius and Brutus, two most noble and illustrious Romans, men of unsurpassable virtue except for one awful sin, [their murder of] Gaius Caesar, who from enemies and opponents made them friends, and from friends was treating them as sons. . . . Antony found Brutus' body, wrapped it in the finest purple garment, burned it, and sent the ashes to his mother, Servilia. Brutus' army, now numbering about 14,000, when they learned of his death sent envoys to Octavian and Antony, who granted them pardon and divided them between their two armies. . . .

Thus did Octavian and Antony by daring danger in two infantry battles achieve a success of a magnitude unequaled by any before it. . . . The army of Octavian and Antony realized their generals' promise, passing in a single day and a single success from the utmost danger of famine and fear of death to lavish wealth, absolute security and glorious victory. And . . . their form of government was also in large measure decided by that day's work, and the Romans never again returned to democracy.

For the Republic, Final Curtain

Dio Cassius, *Roman History*, Book 47, chapter 39

It would be reasonable to consider this the greatest of all the battles that the Romans experienced in their civil wars, not that it surpassed all others in the number and valor of the combatants (for in many places battles had been fought by larger numbers and better men), but because then as never before the battle was over liberty and democracy. It is true that later, just as before, two sides again fell upon each other, but those battles were fought over who should be master while on this occasion one side was leading toward absolutism while the other espoused self-rule. As a result the people never regained complete freedom of speech, even though conquered by no foreign army: as the subject and allied contingents then present were really extensions of the citizen army, the people emerged victors over and losers unto themselves, self-defeating and self-defeated, thus eroding the democratic forces and strengthening the monarchic. But I do not say that it was not to their advantage to be defeated then, for — what better way to describe the two contending sides? — the vanquished were Romans and the victor was [Octavian] Caesar, and the former could no longer remain united under the existing form of government. It is in fact impossible for a pure democracy to govern well when it has expanded into such a massive bulk of empire.

The Wave of the Future

Inscriptiones Latinae Selectae no. 76
On a statue base erected at Saticula in Samnium ca. 40 B.C. It is staggering to reflect how many thousands of similar statues and inscriptions must have been dedicated to Octavian/Augustus in the ensuing half-century of his rule.

To Gaius Julius Caesar son of Gaius, imperator, triumvir for restoring the republic, our patron. [Erected] by decree of the chief magistrates.

Description of Plates

Cover

The reverse of a silver coin [denarius] that was issued by Brutus in 43-42 B.C. It shows the pileus, or cap symbolizing liberty [see note 49], between two daggers. Below is the legend EID·MAR, the archaic spelling of Ides beginning with EI being in all probability a deliberate touch intended to recall the great republican past that the assassins of Caesar claimed to be restoring.

Plate I. Head of Pompey, thought to be a later copy of the one at whose pedestal Caesar was assassinated. Portraits of Alexander the Great are said to have provided the stylistic model, but according to Plutarch the resemblance was more imaginary than real.

Plate II. Head of Cicero, in the last years of his life [he died at age 63]. The portrait is notable for the realism of its details.

Plate III. Caesar in military garb. Numerous heads of Caesar have survived from antiquity. Twenty years ago a noted scholar professed to find in the different extant portraits a score of different attitudes and emotions: majesty, pride, disdain, reflection, prudence, boldness, tension, spirituality, delicacy, fortune, culture, humor, love, cruelty, grief, cheer, clemency, temperance and ferocity. The reader will have to decide for himself which, if any, of these is exhibited by the statue in Plate III.

Plate IV. A Roman bireme of the first century B.C., carrying a contingent of marines. Like the statue in Plate III, this relief is an important source of our knowledge of Roman military costume. The crocodile on the prow suggests that the relief may depict one of Mark Antony's ships which fled to Egypt after the battle at Actium.

Plate V. In 46 B.C. Caesar dedicated the temple of Venus Genetrix — "Venus the Procreatress" [of the Julian clan, according to legend] — in the new forum he was building adjacent to the old to relieve the overcrowding there. The temple, at the west end of the Forum of Julius Caesar, was flanked by colonnades where public and private business would be transacted, and had an equestrian statue of Caesar the dictator in front of its entrance. The reconstruction shown here was drawn in 1934 by Olindo Grossi, then a fellow of the American Academy in Rome, now a practicing architect in New York.

Plate VI. Coins of the period. Under the Republic coins were issued at Rome by a board of three [tresviri monetales] appointed annually for the purpose. The name of one or another of the board usually appears on the coin. Generals in the field also had the right to issue coins as needed, a function they usually delegated to a staff officer, who might put his own or his general's name on the coin.

For the reader's convenience the coins in this plate are shown twice actual size.

1. A gold coin issued in 61[?] B.C.
   Obverse. Encircled in a laurel wreath [symbolizing victory]: a female head, draped in an elephant skin to represent Africa; to the left the word MAGNVS above a sacrificial jug; to the right, a military trumpet.
   Reverse. Pompey, holding a wreath, stands in a chariot drawn by four horses, on one of which sits his son; above them flies Victory, also holding a wreath; below, PRO·COS [= proconsul].

2. Denarius, 54 B.C., celebrating the imminent onset of Crassus' war against Parthia.
   Obverse. A head of Venus adorned with diadem, laurel wreath, earrings, necklace and jewels; to the left, S·C [= "by decree of the senate"].
   Reverse. A soldier holds a spear in his left hand and leads a horse by the bridle with his right; at his feet, a shield and a trophy of military victory; above,

P·CRAS-SVS M·F [="Publius. Crassus, son of Marcus" (the triumvir)].

3. Denarius, 44 B.C.

Obverse. A tetrastyle temple with a globe in the pediment and its doors closed [symbolizing peace throughout the world]; legend, CLEMENTIAE CAESARIS [= "(dedicated to) the clemency of Caesar".

Reverse. A rider steers two galloping horses; behind him, a wreath; legend, P. SERVILIVS MACER.

4. Denarius, 44 B.C.

Obverse. Head of Caesar wearing a laurel wreath; legend, CAESAR DICT·PERPETVO.

Reverse. A caduceus crossed by fasces; in the quadrants, two right hands clasped, a globe, an axe; legend, L.BVCA.

5. Denarius, 43-42 B.C.

Obverse. A head of Liberty; legend, LEIBERTAS. [On the old spelling with EI see the cover photograph.]

Reverse. A lyre between a plectrum and a laurel branch [symbolizing a paean for the victory of liberty]; legend, CAEPIO·BRVTVS·PRO·COS. [For this name of Brutus see note 80.]

Notes

1. J.P.V.D. Balsdon, *Gnomon* 51 [1979], p. 69.
2. This and the longer quotation that ends the paragraph are from Z. Yavetz, *Harvard Studies in Classical Philology* 78 [1974], p. 57.
3. "There were those who, following Mommsen, tended to explain Roman history in terms of the nineteenth century. The conflict of Optimates and Populares tended to be assimilated to the forms of conflict in parliamentary countries; parties, programmes, even democrats and conservatives were brought in" — A.N. Sherwin-White, *Journal of Roman Studies* 46 [1956], p. 1.
4. "Shoemaker, stick to your last" in the popular modern paraphrase, but literally, "shoemaker, no higher than the shoe!" According to a story told in Pliny's *Natural History*, the remark was uttered by the famous painter Apelles when a shoemaker, after rendering an unfavorable judgment on the depiction of a sandal, went on to criticize the rest of the painting.
5. Cicero peppers his letters to Atticus — a connoisseur, as his surname commemorates, of Greek literature — with Greek words and phrases. To attempt to convey the effect, these are rendered in French in this book.
6. Atticus would of course know that the reference here is to the epic poem that Cicero composed celebrating the heroic deeds of his consulship. However it may have served Cicero's vanity and political purposes, the poem was apparently a piece of fustian. Juvenal [*Satire* 10 verse 122] quotes a pompous line from it, and adds,

"He could have disregarded Antony's swords if everything he said was like that."

7. *Iliad* Book 12, verse 243.
8. Cf. p. 23.
9. The Sierra de la Estrella, in present-day Portugal.
10. According to an oft-repeated anecdote, Crassus was
    fond of saying that no one could be considered rich
    who could not maintain a legion out of his annual
    income.
11. Plutarch here echoes Aristotle's classic definition of
    the slave as an *organon empsychon*: "A slave is a living
    tool, but a tool is an inanimate slave" [*Nichomachean
    Ethics*, Book 8, chapter 11; similarly in his *Politics*, Book
    1, chapter 4].
12. This is clearly Cicero's own, probably wishful, estimate
    of the situation.
13. In a slightly earlier letter [no. 19] Cicero tells of Pom-
    pey's being hissed and lampooned in the theater and
    of Caesar's entrance being greeted with silence.
14. In order to prevent the holding of the elections, in
    which Clodius was a candidate for aedile.
15. See note 6, above.
16. Cicero quotes this in Greek from Euripides' *Hippolytus*,
    verse 436.
17. Present-day Rimini, on the Adriatic coast. Unlike Plu-
    tarch and Suetonius [pp. 22, 21] Dio does not dram-
    atize the crossing of the Rubicon, which amounted to
    an invasion of Italy. In this he follows Caesar himself,
    who, in his *Civil War* [Book 1 chapters 7-8], slurs over
    the symbolism of the crossing, saying merely that he
    addressed his troops and "when they cried out that
    they were ready to avenge the wrongs done their im-
    perator . . . he led them to Ariminum."
18. The ruins of the building may still be seen at Ravenna.
19. "Let the die be cast," as quoted by Plutarch [p. 23],
    is the accurate form of the ancient expression.
20. Suetonius and Dio Cassius record this dream as having
    occurred seventeen years earlier, when Caesar was
    quaestor in Spain. The dream was interpreted as prom-

ising him a glorious future, with mother Earth under his sway.

21. Originating in the Greek city-states, these were by now traditional revolutionary slogans.
22. Euripides, *Phoenician Women*, verse 506.
23. *Iliad*, Book 6, verse 442, which Cicero quotes in Greek, using "Trojans" here to refer to the Romans, their descendants according to legend. Vergil adapted Homer's words in the oft-quoted line, *timeo Danaos et dona ferentes* — "I fear the Greeks even bearing gifts" [*Aeneid*, Book 2, verse 49].
24. See note 28.
25. Here Cicero refers to, and in what follows quotes from, his *Republic*, a treatise on the ideal state modeled on Plato.
26. I.e., Pompey had threatened to regard those of his supporters who stayed behind as enemies: cf. p. 25 [above].
27. Coupled with Cicero's rhetorical question in the preceding letter about the possibility of his going over to Caesar's side, this disingenuous answer suggests that "feelers" were in fact being exchanged through intermediaries. Note too in this connection that in the next paragraph Cicero speaks of enclosing Pompey's letters to him, but does not offer to enclose Caesar's.
28. Tullia was Cicero's daughter [and Dolabella's wife], Terentia his wife.
29. A euphemistic reference to the pardon Cicero would have to obtain from Caesar before he could return to Rome. Cicero was too proud to beg for it, and after Pharsalus Caesar magnanimously invited him to return.
30. Caesar was particularly anxious to win back [cf. pp. 29 - 34, and note 29 above] the support of Cicero, the leading mouthpiece of the optimates. During the next few months, as the following pages show, Cicero adopted an attitude of polite correctness and even moderate cooperativeness, prepared to tolerate a moderate dictatorship of republican cast, if it turned out that way, as a lesser evil than civil war.

159

31. Cicero had a number of trusted Caesarians present in court as character witnesses and interceders for his client.

32. In the paragraph omitted here Cicero reminded Caesar, not at all subtly, of some political assistance — we are in the dark as to the details — rendered him ten years before by Titus Ligarius, one of the brothers.

33. This quotation, which Cicero used also in one of his philosophical works, is from Gaius Lucilius, of the second century B.C., Rome's leading satirist before Horace.

34. I.e., they did not talk politics.

35. For Caecina see p. 44. Pitholaus is recorded as the author of a biography of Pompey, whose freedman he was.

36. The point of this and the following examples is that, in signal honor of Caesar, royal and noble personages played roles usually performed by humbler people and slaves [e.g. gladiators].

37. In the pre-Julian calendar the twelve months totaled 355 days, and every other February an additional short month [ca. 22 days] was intercalated to keep the calendar in tune with the seasons. But the time of intercalation had to be proclaimed by the pontifices, and in the last decades of the Republic they failed to do so with the requisite regularity. As to the motivation of their action or inaction, Cicero makes a passing reference to what he blandly calls their negligence, but other ancient writers call it manipulation and ascribe it to political corruption: after all, omitting the intercalation would shorten a political enemy's term of office by a month.

38. See note 21.

39. Then, as now, wars frequently resulted [inter alia] in inflation of prices.

40. Caesar, and the Roman emperors after him, were afraid that these *collegia*, usually socio-religious associations, might easily become centers of political intrigue.

41. Z. Yavetz, *Harvard Studies in Classical Philology* 78 [1974], p. 62.

42. Not otherwise identifiable.

43. Gaius Trebonius according to most sources, including Plutarch himself in chapter 17 of his *Life of Brutus* [above, p. 66]. The following, from Plutarch's *Life of Mark Antony*, chapter 13, is worth quoting here:

> When Brutus and Cassius were counting up the friends on whom they could rely for the deed, they wondered about Antony. While the rest were for recruiting him, Trebonius was opposed. He had, he said, quietly and discreetly sounded out Antony when they were on their way — traveling together, and even sharing a tent — to meet Caesar on his return from Spain. Antony had understood full well, and had rebuffed his approach; on the other hand, he had not reported it to Caesar but had faithfully kept the story to himself.
>
> It was next proposed to cut down Antony after killing Caesar, but Brutus blocked that, arguing that an action undertaken in defense of law and justice must be absolutely free of injustice. But as they were afraid of Antony's physical strength and the authority of his high office, it was settled that when Caesar was entering the senate house and the deed was about to be done, some of the conspirators would make it their business to detain Antony outside with conversation on some subject or other.

44. As this province was most strategic because of its proximity to Rome, Caesar would naturally want to keep it in the hands of trusted friends and supporters.

45. I.e., the board of Quindecimviri, who had charge of the Sibylline Books.

46. A law about which we know little except that it apparently ordered statues of Caesar to be erected in every municipality in Italy.

47. In his preface to Book 8, with which he completed Caesar's *Gallic War*, Hirtius addresses Lucius Cornelius Balbus, one of Caesar's closest associates.

48. For examples cf. pp. 29, 31.

49. When slaves were manumitted they were given a cap of a special shape as a sign of their freedom.

50. On these gladiators see p. 63.

51. See Glossary under legatio.

52. The Roman formula for banishment.

53. A euphemism for war.

54. That is, they claimed Caesar's estate for the treasury, and they were afraid — rightly, as events proved — that his will would bequeath it to his heirs and legatees. Octavian, Caesar's heir, did of course subsequently become sole ruler: Appian writes with the wisdom of hindsight.

55. In Roman monetary terms, three hundred sesterces.

56. See note 58.

57. A Roman historian contemporary with Caesar.

58. Of the plays of Pacuvius and Atilius [second century B.C.] only scattered fragments survive in quotations by later writers. Atilius' *Electra* was probably a translation of Sophocles' play with that title.

59. Cf. the two figures that appeared when Caesar crossed the Rubicon.

60. March 17th, when the senate voted to confirm Caesar's acts and to allow a public funeral and the reading out of his will.

61. A quotation from Aeschylus' *Prometheus Bound* [verse 682].

62. Some commentators think the last five words are intended to be ironic. Be that as it may, it is clear that Octavian did not long delay in playing up to Cicero as the elder statesman, and that Cicero was flattered by these attentions from the young Caesar (as he had been by those from the old: see pp. 51 - 52) and thought he could turn them to the political advantage of his own side.

63. The result of Cicero's successful prosecution [in 70 B.C.] of Gaius Verres for inordinate corruption and extortion while governor of Sicily. Cicero's *Verrine Orations* are among his most celebrated.

64. That is, granting them full citizenship, not just the limited "Latin rights."

65. That is, loyal to the cause that Cicero approves.

66. Cicero deliberately chooses this slighting word for Octavian, who was then $18^{1}/_{2}$ years old.

67. See note 60.

68. Pilia was Atticus' wife, Attica his daughter.

69. Cicero means Antony, not Octavian.

70. Lieutenants of Caesar, whom he had designated to be consuls in 43 B.C.

71. Obviously one strengthening the Caesarians' position, perhaps the one giving Antony the command of Cisalpine Gaul and the Macedonian legions.

72. The victory games that Caesar had vowed at Pharsalus to accompany the dedication of his temple to Venus, the legendary ancestress of the Julian house.

73. Tribunes took up their office on the 10th of December.

74. See Glossary under consultum.

75. Thirty-one was the legal minimum age for quaestor, the lowest rung in the traditional Roman ladder of public offices.

76. I.e., the assassination of Caesar.

77. Caesar's law of 59 B.C. [above, p. 59]. Cicero charges elsewhere that Antony had distributed some of the land to certain of his henchmen.

78. Most desirable because very fertile and also close to both Rome and the Bay of Naples area.

79. The reiteration of this provision, made in greater detail in an earlier clause, was no doubt intended to assure the veterans that it was here offered in good faith, since Cicero had in the preceding decades been a consistent opponent of such laws, including the Julian law of 59 B.C. At the same time, Cicero's clever insertion of "without injury to private individuals" would reassure the optimates and their chief supporters, the landed gentry.

80. Marcus Brutus' name after his adoption by Quintus Servilius Caepio, his mother's brother. See the coin reproduced on the cover and Plate VI no. 5.

81. The strategic importance of Syria was that it had the greatest concentration of military forces guarding Rome's eastern frontier.

82. Antony's brother Gaius had fallen into the hands of Brutus, who was not sure what to do with him.

83. Only a free man bore his father's family name. A slave was defined in Roman law as a "son of no father."

84. Modern scholarship has not succeeded in identifying the spot thus described by the ancient writers.

85. A friend and lieutenant of Antony's.

86. This is Appian's loose translation of the official title, *tresviri rei publicae constituendae*, "triumvirs for restoring the republic."

87. See note 86.

88. The usual procedure was to fix a future date.

89. See note 86.

90. = 100,000 sesterces.

91. The customary punishment inflicted when runaway slaves were recaptured.

92. In 31 B.C., after the Battle of Actium.

93. The date was 7 December 43 B.C.

94. Pompey's son Sextus dominated the western Mediterranean till 36 B.C., when he was decisively defeated by Octavian's general Agrippa in a naval battle off Sicily. Lucius Statius Murcus and Gnaeus Domitius Ahenobarbus, anti-Caesarians leading a sizable fleet, controlled the Adriatic at this time.

95. The signal to attack.

Glossary

Consultum ultimum: The "ultimate decree" of the senate was, in effect, a declaration of martial law. First employed against Gaius Gracchus and thereafter some ten times in all [including against Caesar in 49 B.C.], it declared the existence of a public emergency and gave the consuls what amounted to dictatorial powers. Specifically, it instructed them "to see to it that the republic suffered no harm," which was interpreted as authorizing them to exercise any measures of repression they deemed necessary, even if it meant violating the normal rights of Roman citizens.

consularis: The lifelong honorific term for a man who had attained the consulship.

curule chair: Originally made of [or adorned with] ivory, it served as a symbol of the offices of aedile, praetor, consul, dictator and censor. Attainment of one of these curule magistracies elevated a man and all his descendants to the class of nobles.

denarius: A Roman coin, weighing in Caesar's day about 4 gr. of silver [which was worth about one U.S. dollar in 1984].

drachma: see talent.

free embassy: see legatio libera.

genius: The vital spirit inherent in or attendant upon each freeborn man, and worshipped as his guardian. After Caesar it became the focus of the worship of the living emperor.

imperator: Originally the honorary appellative of a victorious general, it was taken as a permanent title first by Caesar and after him by the Roman rulers [principes] beginning with Augustus, whom we, as a result, call by the Anglicized form "emperors."

interregnum: Obviously originating in the period of the monarchy, this term under the republic designated a time when

165

— owing to death, postponed elections, or other causes — there were no consuls in office.

legatio libera: The "free embassy" was an unofficial mission authorizing a senator to absent himself from Rome at public expense, usually to see to some private matters.

martial law: see consultum ultimum.

optimates: "The best men" was the term arrogated to themselves by the conservatives of the republican oligarchy and their political supporters. With the Gracchi there emerged an opposition coalition known as populares.

pomerium: The religiously ordained and hence involate area within the boundary of the original city of Rome, it was progressively extended by Sulla, Caesar, and several of the emperors to symbolize their extension of the boundaries of the empire.

populares: see optimates.

rostra: The speaker's platform in the Roman forum was so called because the original structure was adorned with the prows [rostra] of the Volscian ships captured in the fourth century B.C. A new structure was begun by Caesar and completed by Augustus.

sesterce: A Roman coin, $= \frac{1}{4}$ denarius.

talent: This Greek unit, originally a weight, equaled 6,000 drachmas. The drachma was equated with the Roman denarius.

ultimate decree: see consultum ultimum.

For Further Reading

The literature is enormous: close to 20,000 books and articles in the last fifty years alone. Following is a selection of writings in English.

Adcock, F.E. *Caesar as Man of Letters*. Cambridge, 1956.

Balsdon, J.P.V.D. "The Ides of March," in *Historia* 7 [1958], pp. 80-94.

_____ . *Julius Caesar: A Political Biography*. New York, 1967 [published the same year in London under the title *Julius Caesar and Rome*].

Carcopino, J. *Cicero: The Secrets of his Correspondence*. New Haven, 1951. A provocative, entertaining account by a hostile witness.

Clarke, M.L. *The Noblest Roman. Marcus Brutus and his Reputation*. London, 1981.

Collins, J. H. "Caesar and the Corruption of Power," in *Historia* 4 [1955], pp. 445-65.

Frisch, H. *Cicero's Fight for the Republic: The Historical Background of Cicero's Philippics*. Copenhagen, 1946.

Fuller, J.F.C. *Julius Caesar: Man, Soldier and Tyrant*. New Brunswick, 1965. Primarily an analysis of Caesar's military actions, by a retired army careerist.

Gelzer, M. *Caesar, Politician and Statesman*. Oxford, 1968 [translation of the sixth German edition, 1959; the first edition appeared in 1921]. Has been called "the fullest and best modern life of Caesar, fully documented."

Grant, M. *Julius Caesar*. New York, 1969. A popular work by a noted scholar, lavishly illustrated.

Greenhalgh, P. *Pompey*. 2 vols. London, 1980, 1981. The closest thing we have to a definitive account.

Gruen, E.S. *The Last Generation of the Roman Republic*. Berkeley, 1974.

_____ . "Pompey, the Roman Aristocracy and the Conference at Luca," in *Historia* 18 [1969], pp. 71-108.

Heaton, J.W. *Mob Violence in the Late Roman Republic*. Urbana, 1939.

Holmes, T.R. *The Roman Republic*. 3 vols. Oxford, 1923. Our most detailed account of the last decades of the Republic.

_____ . *The Architect of the Roman Empire*, Vol. I. Oxford, 1928. An equally detailed account of the events following the Ides of March.

Huzar, E.G. *Mark Antony: A Biography*. Minneapolis, 1978.

Lindsay, J. *Marc Antony: his World and his Contemporaries*. New York, 1937. A well-informed popularization, breezy in style, with emphasis on "the motives of the protagonists."

Luibheid, C. "The Luca Conference," in *Classical Philology* 65 [1970], pp. 88-94.

Radin, M. *Marcus Brutus*. New York, 1939. A biography of "an incurably cleft soul," torn between personal preference and duty.

Ridley, R.T. "The Extraordinary Commands of the Late Republic," in *Historia* 30 [1981], pp. 280-97.

Seager, R. *Pompey: a Political Biography*. Berkeley, 1979.

Syme, R. *The Roman Revolution*. Oxford, 1939. A classic work, both in its contents and in its Tacitean style.

Taylor, L.R. *Party Politics in the Age of Caesar*. Berkeley, 1949.

Weinstock, S. *Divus Iulius*. Oxford, 1971. The last word on the question of divine honors.

Yavetz, Z. "Caesar, Caesarism, and Historians," in *Journal of Contemporary History* 6 no. 2 [1971], pp. 184-201.

_____ . *"Existimatio, Fama*, and the Ides of March," in *Harvard Studies in Classical Philology* 78 [1974], pp. 35-65.

_____ . *Plebs and Princeps*. Oxford, 1969.

_____ . *Julius Caesar and his Public Image*. Ithaca, 1983.

THE
IDES OF
MARCH

PLATE I

PLATE II

PLATE III

22

PLATE IV

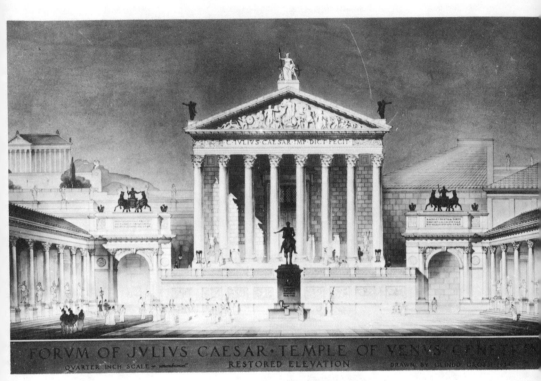

FORVM OF JVLIVS CAESAR · TEMPLE OF VENVS GENETRIX
QVARTER INCH SCALE   RESTORED ELEVATION   DRAWN BY GLINDO GROSSI 1934

PLATE V

PLATE VI

PLATE VI
continued